THE SACRAMENT OF THE WORD

Donald Coggan was born in London in October 1909, and educated at Merchant Taylors' School, St John's College, Cambridge and Wycliffe Hall, Oxford.

In 1931 he became Assistant Lecturer in Semitic Languages and Literature at Manchester University, and three years later took up his first curacy, at St Mary's Church, Islington. In 1937 he went to Canada, where he was professor at Wycliffe College, Toronto, returning to England in 1944 to become Principal of the London College of Divinity. In 1956 he became Bishop of Bradford, and later Archbishop of York (1961-74).

In 1974 Dr Coggan became the one hundred and first Archbishop of Canterbury, a position he held until 1980.

His leisure interests include gardening, motoring and music, and he is the author of numerous books, including *The Heart of the Christian Faith* (also published by Fount Paperbacks). His wife, Jean, is an author in her own right. The Coggans have two grown-up daughters.

By the same author
available from Fount Paperbacks

The Heart of the Christian Faith

Donald Coggan

The Sacrament of the Word

Donald Coggan.

Collins
FOUNT PAPERBACKS

First published in Great Britain in 1987 by Fount Paperbacks, London

Copyright © Donald Coggan 1987

Made and printed in Great Britain by
William Collins Sons & Co. Ltd, Glasgow

In gratitude to two men, whose care for preaching
informs and inspires others in their ministry –

DOUGLAS CLEVERLEY FORD

Hon. Director, The College of Preachers, England (1960-1973);
Six Preacher, Canterbury Cathedral,

and

CHARLES JACKSON MINIFIE

President, The College of Preachers, Washington, U.S.A.

Contents

Foreword

Why is the sermon in many Anglican churches today so often short on substance, shallow in understanding, and shaky in presentation? Why do many preachers spend time answering unreal questions people never ask, or asking real questions but never trying to answer them?

Bishop Donald is well aware of the kind of reasons usually given. Defeatism – the belief that in today's world of news snippets and TV images people just won't listen to fifteen minutes of the serious spoken word; lack of reading, reflection and preparation time in the modern minister's life of perpetual motion; the loss of the "bi-focal" tradition in Anglicanism, dedicated to both the biblical Word and the Gospel Sacraments. These and other similar factors are kindly but sharply observed. (One I would add myself is fear of exercising spiritual authority.)

Why should this be when, as Bishop Donald constantly reminds us, there are plenty of excellent books on preaching, and training is given in theological colleges and, one hopes, in a minister's first post?

The fundamental cause is something much deeper than practical difficulties, cultural resistance or techniques of communication. It is a loss of vision – the vision of the Gospel, and of the unique role of the preacher in serving that Gospel. It is the glory of this book and its very special value that, while also supplying much practical wisdom, it begins from this vision and never loses it.

Bishop Gregory the Great once wrote: "It is for love of him", that is, God, "that I do not spare myself in preaching him." Bishop Donald leads us to this quotation as the deepest motive of the preacher's work, but also adds the vital complementary thought, "It is for love of *them*", that is, God's people, "that I do not spare myself in preaching him." The preacher's primary agenda are God, Christ, the Holy Spirit, Incarnation, Cross, Resurrection, the Creation, redemption and fulfilment of all things, and, springing from the teaching and commending of this supreme Good News, the imperatives for our involvement in the world. Within this perspective, I believe, questions of biblical criticism and exposition, which are not Bishop Donald's concern here, can in fact be creatively and positively handled. The preacher stands at the intersection of the eternal and the temporal, to be sanctified by saving truth so that others may receive Him who is the Truth, and take Him into the complex problems and agonies of our world.

That is why this book is called *The Sacrament of the Word*. It is about the imparting of Christ through our words, and so inevitably through ourselves. I have myself been greatly helped and challenged by it at many points. It is a special privilege to be able in its very pages to express my gratitude, which I know will be shared by many readers – not only those who will hear Bishop Donald's well-loved voice on every page, but those who come to him for the first time.

The book itself is the best demonstration of its own message. May God bless it richly to the revival of authentic preaching in our day.

Eastertide 1987 +John Sarum

Introduction

In writing this book I have had in mind both clergy and laity; those who occupy the pulpit and those who sit in the pew. I have done so in the conviction that preaching is a combined operation, only properly achieved when there is a lively reciprocity, a relationship at work, between the man or woman in the pulpit doing the speaking and the men and women in the pew doing — what? Well, that is the question. Sleeping? Enduring? Hoping for the end? or — ? The questions deserve at least an examination.

The book springs from a conviction that it is largely for lack of an understanding of what Christian preaching *is*, and of the part played in it by preacher and congregation, that the Sacrament of the Word has fallen on bad days. It is often said that the days of great preaching are gone, and that is made an excuse for relegating preaching to a place of minor importance in the life and worship of the Church — "a few sentences from the chancel steps will do". It is true that the days when the sermon was the main event in the weekly life of a community are gone for ever: there are counter-attractions in plenty today, and other means of communication such as the press, radio and television of which previous generations knew little or nothing. It may well be that the days of the great orators, too, are gone for ever: it would be difficult to find many such in the Church, or in the legal profession, or in politics. But to succumb to the temptation of thinking that preaching matters little, and that a short chat, hastily thought up and indifferently delivered, will do, is to do despite to a major biblical insight and to fly in the face of the age-long teaching of the Church in general and of the Ordinal in particular.

I am fully aware of the fact that preaching is only a small sector of the whole circle occupied by the communication of the

13

Gospel. That Gospel is communicated most powerfully and most frequently by sheer *love* − love shown by the parish priest in his visiting, and by the everyday intercourse of Christians with people whom they meet socially or at work. Such communication of the Gospel often takes place "without a word being said", as Peter put it when he wrote to wives about their disbelieving husbands who are "won over . . . by observing the . . . behaviour of their wives" (1 Peter 3:1). Hands, as well as lips, can, and constantly do, convey the Gospel. And when a word is said, it will be, as often as not, a quite informal "gossiping of the Gospel" which will prove the most effective way of continuing the evangelistic work of the Church.

I am aware, also, that the world of the late twentieth century has passed largely from a word culture into an image culture − the Christian message must be presented *visually*, by means of drama, television, and so on, if it is to gain access to mind and conscience today.

Does this mean, then, that virtually no place is left for the public ministry of the word through preaching? It is true that only a small part of our population will be touched by this particular method of communication. But two things must be borne in mind. **First,** even though in the largely paganized West the percentage of people who go to church is much smaller than in, say, Africa or parts of Latin America, those who do so still represent a very considerable part of the community. Even in Britain, more people are to be found in church on any given Sunday than were present in the football stadium the previous Saturday. This must never be forgotten. It presents a unique field of opportunity and influence.

Secondly, the part of the community who do go to church with some degree of regularity is an *influential* minority. It consists of people serious enough in mind and purpose to devote time and attention to the things of the Spirit in an age when such things are largely neglected. Such men and women deserve the best that can be given them.

It is to these people, clergy and laity, that this book is addressed. It is with this facet of Christian communication that we are concerned − the actual task of preaching and of that discussion and dialogue which, as we shall argue, should ideally follow it. Canon Bryan Green, who has exercised an influential world-wide ministry over many years, has recently emphasized the present-day importance of preaching: "The Sunday sermon is still the opportunity . . . for teaching the majority of our church congregation the truths of the Christian Gospel. Only a very small minority of them are willing to experience any Christian education other than that, either on their own by reading or by taking some special course."

Preaching still remains a powerful means of communicating the Gospel in a highly secularized society. Failure to appreciate that fact and to seize the opportunity which preaching presents is playing a large part in the weakness of the Church's ministry today.

In recent decades much care has been given to liturgical revision, and the Church has been greatly enriched thereby. The time has come for clergy and laity together to think again about preaching. This book aims, in some small way, to stimulate such thinking. Only incidentally does it touch on the "mechanics" of preaching.

For many years, I have written and lectured on this subject, always as one engaged myself in the battle. For battle it is — against innate laziness, against the surrounding secularization of society, against " spiritual wickedness in high places". But what a challenge preaching presents! Yes, and what fun it can be to battle, and to overcome, and to have the joy of seeing on the faces of those who listen an expression that says: "Is the Christian message *really* like that? It is too good to be true!"

I have been anxious not to clutter the book with too many references to the immense literature which has grown up around the subject of preaching. My indebtedness to much of it will be apparent to those who have read widely on the subject. I have, however, given fairly full Scripture references, in the hope that readers may wish to follow them up in their further study.

I am grateful to S.P.C.K. for allowing me to make use of material in my small book *On Preaching* (1978); to Hodder & Stoughton, for similar permission in my *Stewards of Grace* (1958; second impression 1962); to the Lutterworth Press, in my

The Ministry of the Word (1945; revised edition 1964); and to the London Baptist Preachers'' Association for permission to use in chapter 2 part of my lecture *He has spoken through the Prophets* (1985).

I am grateful to John Baker, Bishop of Salisbury and until recently Chairman of the Doctrine Commission of the Church of England, for his kindness in writing a Foreword, and, above all, for his friendship; and to Professor C.F.D. Moule who was good enough to read the first draft of the book and to make a number of valuable criticisms and suggestions. He must not be blamed for my own errors and inadequacies. I thank Mrs Tremenheere for her patience and typing skill.

Take thou Authority to preach the Word of God, and to minister the Holy Sacraments . . .

The Book of Common Prayer: The Ordinal

1

A Preacher's Dream

On Tuesday, 2 April 1985, my wife and I had the unforgettable experience of seeing the Grand Canyon for the first time. That night I dreamed. On waking, I was so haunted by the dream that I determined not to allow it to fade from my memory, as dreams so often do.

I dreamed that once again I was a diocesan bishop. One of my clergy — I can recall no name or parish — was arranging a date when I would visit his church and preach. "When", he said, "can you come and give us a paper?" I laughed at the phrase he used, but the laughter was mixed with a kind of horror. The vicar simply explained that that was the phrase used in his parish when his people referred to preaching — "giving a paper".

I did not sleep much more that night. I kept turning over in my mind that extraordinary phrase — "giving a paper".

What in fact is the difference between reading a paper to an audience and preaching to a congregation? One has heard sermons which were precisely *that* — the giving of a paper, probably prepared with meticulous care, but that and nothing more. Is *that* preaching? If not, wherein lies the difference?

As I lay in bed thinking about my dream, it occurred to me how strange it was that preaching should have been the subject of it. Why not the Grand Canyon, which had filled my mind and caught my imagination and held me spellbound during the hours of the previous day? The activities of the mind during sleep are passing strange.

Then it came to me that perhaps there was a connection. As I stood and viewed the Canyon or looked at it through the windows of the aeroplane which traversed it, I wondered how I could convey anything worthwhile about it to one who had never seen it. Suppose I wanted to share with him something of its immensity, its awesomeness, the sternness of the reds of the rock-strata, the infinite gentleness of the yellows and greens which flowed together in graceful skirts of beauty, the power of the river which over countless millennia had carved its way through the rocks and which moved a mile below us defying comprehension. How would I find words adequate to convey the thing which had assaulted mind and eye during that sunny spring day? Or how could my wife, skilled with her paints, capture and convey a fraction of what she had seen?

The connection between the experience at the Grand Canyon on the one hand, and the task of preaching on the other, became steadily clearer. The fact of the Christian revelation stands, like some great canyon, defying comprehension or explanation or exposition. Before it we can only kneel in awe and adoration. God, "source, guide and goal of all that is", revealed in Christ incarnate, crucified, risen, the One in whom all things cohere and towards whom all things move — there he stands, unchanging, eternal, dwelling in light unapproachable. How can one *say* anything about that? Is not silence, the silence of worship, all that can be engaged in? Frederick Buechner* writes of "truth that cannot finally be understood but only experienced", truth that can best be entered into in silence. "Be silent and know that I am God" (Psalm 46:10). But out of the silence comes the word; and the preacher, just because he is a preacher, must seek to convey something of what he has seen, something of the awesome strength, the tender beauty, the compelling glory of the "many-splendoured thing" which is the Gospel. The vision was given him to give again. The truth must be shared even though it cannot fully be grasped.

Precisely in this is the demand of preaching, the tyranny and the loveliness of the thing. You cannot, in the pulpit, "give a paper" about that. You can give a life to its exposition and to its commendation.

In doing so, you will know the stress and experience, the grace which are part and parcel of this task of mammoth proportions.

---

* In a remarkable chapter of his book, *Telling the Truth: The Gospel as Tragedy, Comedy and Fairy Tale* (Harper & Row, 1977), p. 21.

That is what this book is about.
But where to begin?

*

Within the wide family of the Anglican Communion, at the heart
of the service of consecration (of a bishop) or ordination (of a
priest), a little drama of great importance is unfailingly enacted.
It takes the form of a gift. There is handed to the newly
consecrated bishop or newly ordained priest a book, and that
book is a Bible. According to the use of the Episcopal Church of
the United States of America, the Bible is presented to the new
bishop with these words:

> "Receive the Holy Scriptures. Feed the flock of Christ
> committed to your charge, guard and defend them in his truth,
> and be a faithful steward of his holy Word and Sacraments".

To the new priest, the bishop says:

> "Receive this Bible as a sign of the authority given you to
> preach the Word of God and to administer his holy Sacra-
> ments. Do not forget the trust committed to you as a priest of
> the Church of God."

When, some years later, that same priest is inducted into the
charge of a parish, representatives of the congregation present
him with a Bible, saying:

> "N., accept this Bible, and be among us . . . as one who
> proclaims the Word."

Within the Church of England, the same symbolic act is performed. In the *Alternative Services Book 1980*, the words which
accompany it are even more specific. To the new Bishop, the
Archbishop says:

> "Receive this book; here are words of eternal life. Take them

for your guide, and declare them to the world. Keep watch over the whole flock in which the Holy Spirit has appointed you shepherd. Encourage the faithful, restore the lost, build up the body of Christ; that when the Chief Shepherd shall appear, you may receive the unfading crown of glory."

To the new priest, the Bishop says:

"Receive this Book, as a sign of the authority which God has given you this day to preach the Gospel of Christ and to minister his Holy Sacraments."

Even more impressive and weighty, as some may think, are the words of the Prayer Book of 1662. To the new Bishop, the Archbishop says as he hands him the Bible:

"Give heed unto reading, exhortation, and doctrine. Think upon the things contained in this Book. Be diligent in them, that the increase coming thereby may be manifest unto all men. Take heed unto thyself, and to doctrine, and be diligent in them: for by so doing thou shalt both save thyself and them that hear thee. Be to the flock of Christ a shepherd, not a wolf; feed them, devour them not. Hold up the weak, seek the lost. Be so merciful, that you be not too remiss; so minister discipline, that you forget not mercy: that when the chief Shepherd shall appear you may receive the never-fading crown of glory; through Jesus Christ our Lord."

To the new priest, the Bishop says:

"Take thou Authority to preach the Word of God, and to minister the Holy Sacraments in the Congregation, where thou shalt be lawfully appointed thereunto."

Similarly, when a new Reader is admitted to office, he or she is given a Bible (or New Testament) by the Bishop or Archdeacon, before the scarf is placed upon the shoulders of the candidate. Against this background of symbolism, there can be no doubt as to the importance which the churches of the Anglican Communion attach to the ministry of the Word. It is wholly consonant with the doctrine of the Articles of the Church of England: "The visible Church of Christ is a congregation of faithful men, in the which the pure Word of God is preached, and the Sacraments be duly administered . . . " (Article XIX), and with their declaration that "holy Scripture containeth all things necessary to salvation: so that whatsoever is not read therein, nor may be proved thereby, is not to be required of any man, that it should be believed as an article of the Faith, or be thought requisite or necessary to salvation" (Article VI).

The presentation of this book to a man or woman, at this critical point in his or her life, does not in itself presuppose or demand a particular adherence to any one theory of inspiration. It makes no statement about literal or liberal interpretation. But it clearly regards the Bible as the bearer of certain facts, certain doctrines, certain emphases with which the person who receives the book is put in trust — to receive, to ponder, to hand on, to expound. This book, to use Martin Luther's apt parable, is the "cradle" that bears the Christ to us. Elsewhere, he likens the Bible to the swaddling-clothes in which the infant Jesus was laid: "Poor and mean are the swaddling-clothes, but precious is the Treasure, Christ, that lives therein." Christ is its central figure who holds the book together, and without whom it makes no sense. We do not worship the book. We are not bibliolators. We worship the God who speaks, the Christ who is the Word, the Spirit who guides the Church in the true interpretation of the Scriptures and applies its truths to the hearts and consciences of its readers.

The architectural arrangements and furnishings of a church building should clearly show to the eye the centrality both of the Word and of the Sacraments. Anyone entering a church should at once be arrested by two things — the central importance of a table where the faithful are fed sacramentally and of a pulpit (and/or lectern) from which the Word is read and expounded. Emphasis on the one should not lead to the disparagement of the other, nor vice versa. True Anglicanism — I would dare to say, a true presentation of the Christian faith — is bi-focal. Let me make my point by telling of an incident in my own experience which has left a permanent impression on my mind.

In the course of my work as Archbishop of York, I had occasion to go to a certain town in the Province which had as its main glory an ancient church. The incumbent, with commendable vigour, had raised a large sum of money to refashion the church, to restore it to something of its former glory, and to adapt it for greater usefulness under modern conditions. I was to preach at a Eucharist at its rehallowing. The greatest possible care had been put into the preparation of the service. Architecturally, the central feature was the altar, central and resplendent. There could be no doubt that the Church of England was a sacramental church, nor where it was that her children should kneel to be fed. The architect, the craftsmen, the silversmiths, all had given of their best. There was one focus. You could not miss it.

"This is very fine, Vicar. You have done magnificently. Now – you have asked me to preach. *Where do I preach from*?" "They will bring you in a little stand, Archbishop, when the time comes." And they did. A poor, paltry thing it was, liable to collapse if by chance I leaned upon it, the sort of temporary contraption from which any man might have scorned to give out the notices of the week. This was to be the thing from which the everlasting Gospel was to be proclaimed. As soon as the sermon was over, it was taken away into oblivion. And good riddance, too!

The service over, I was introduced to the distinguished architect. I complimented him on so much that was good in the work that he had done. But while I was musing the fire had kindled. Then spake I with my tongue. "When will you ecclesiastical architects", I said, "give us *Anglican* ecclesiastical architecture? Is it not time that a visitor from some other tradition than ours should be able to see, by the very architecture and furnishing of the building, that Anglicanism is "bi-focal" in its means of grace, that the living God comes to us both in the Sacrament of the Body and Blood of Christ *and* in the Sacrament of the Word?" "Yes", said the architect, in reply to my protest and distress. "Yes, I see what you mean. I appreciate the point. I did in fact talk it over with the Vicar. But he said there was no need for a pulpit. He just speaks off the cuff."

Three months later I went on holiday to Sweden. I visited its churches. I could not read or speak its language. What would the architecture of the churches tell me about its theology? This is what I found: great honour was obviously done to the Sacrament of the Body and Blood of Christ. The altars of these churches were ornate and lavish in their accoutrements. Above them were figures — the Father in his almightiness, the Son in his passion, Moses with his commandments, and Aaron with his censer, saints, apostles, martyrs in goodly array. There was no doubt about the importance of the Eucharist if we were to judge by what the architects and craftsmen had to say. And what about the Sacrament of the Word? Here again was magnificence — a throne indeed! And immediately above the head of the preacher, suspended from the elaborate sounding-board, as often as not was the figure of the Dove, symbol of the Holy Spirit, eloquent of the fact that in the ministry of the Word, *God* is at work; this is no mere man prating.

I contrasted what I had seen in that town in my Province — and I noted that what I saw there was repeated in all too many English churches — with what I saw in Sweden. And I asked myself, if a complete stranger to English and to Swedish worship were to come, without further instruction, to see the churches of these two countries, what would he deduce as to their respective theologies of Word and Sacrament? I think the answer is clear; and I am distressed.

Do not let me be misunderstood. I am not, of course, suggesting that for an effective ministry of Word or Sacrament an elaborate setting is called for. That is not my point. All that is needed for the first is a man of God, a congregation, and the Bible. All that is needed for the second is a celebrant, a congregation, a bottle of wine and a loaf of bread. There may or may not be elaborations on that theme. What I am asking is whether, from the point of view of architecture, that particular instance of English arrangement or the Swedish balance of Word and Sacrament the better sets out the truth of the New Testament. I have no doubt about the answer.

The central doctrines of the Church should be taught by the

eye as well as by the ear. The Spirit knocks for entrance at eye-gate as well as ear-gate. Let ecclesiastical architects and church furnishers take note, and thus aid him in his work!

And let this be added: Those who are responsible for the training of tomorrow's clergy — do they give their students as thorough a grounding in the theology of the Word as they do in the theology of the Sacraments? Maybe there are some colleges to whose teachers the question should be put the other way round — do their students have an adequate training in sacramental theology? But at the moment, we are concerned with the provision of such a deep and thorough theology of the Word as will compel the occupant of the pulpit to exercise his craft with awe and deep reverence and, so long as he lives, to give all that is in him (and all that the Spirit provides) to the fulfilment of a lively ministry of the Word.

The preacher himself must be — and must be seen to be — both a hearer and a servant of the Word of God. He is a man under authority, and he has an authority not his own. He will approach his task with awe, mindful of the exclamation of Donald Cargill the Covenanter, from the foot of the gallows before his execution: "Lord knows I go up this ladder with less fear and perturbation than ever I entered a pulpit to preach." He will approach his task also with quiet confidence. After all, he is not going at his own charges; "faithful is he who calls you."

Good Master, my only Master, thou who from my youth up hast taught me until this day all that I ever learned of the truth, thou, my way, my end, lead me also unto thy end. Show to thy little child, how to solve the knot of thy word.

From a prayer of Archbishop Bradwardine
(Archbishop of Canterbury, d.1349)

"As the Lord lives . . . I will say only what the Lord tells me to say."

1 Kings 22:14

2
The Old Testament Background

The only valid starting point for thinking about preaching is thinking about God. A healthy doctrine of preaching springs from a healthy theology, as surely as good fruit comes from a good tree. Begin with an inadequate or feeble doctrine of God's word and the pulpit utterance will be feeble. Before long, the preacher will experience aridity, an attack of "the sickness that destroys at the noon-day" of his ministry (if not before), a diminishing of enthusiasm. He will be a merchant of words, words without power, words without grace, a deliverer of essays, a reader of "papers". The world has plenty of such already; we should not add to their number. We dare not trivialize preaching.

What, then, do we believe about God? Can that belief be stated clearly, even in monosyllables? Is there a foundation to preaching so deep, so profound, that, without depriving it of its essential meaning, we can so put it that an intelligent layman, ignorant of theological terms, can appreciate what we are engaged in when we preach? Heeding the warning of C.S. Lewis that "many writers on 'religion' . . . have a positive love for the smudgy and the polysyllabic", let us at least have a try. Thought should not be clothed in pure wool!

Christians believe in a *God who speaks*. Ours is not a silent God, a God who sits, Sphinx-like, looking out unblinking on a world in agony. The God depicted in the Bible is the God of creation, who spoke and darkness gave way to light, chaos to order; the God of redemption, whose "Word was made flesh and dwelt among us . . . full of grace and truth"; the God of the book of the Revelation where the Spirit and the Bride say "Come". The God who speaks breaks into history, "interferes" in the destinies of men and women.

If we ask: "Why is the Christian's God a God who speaks?",

31

the answer must be: "He speaks *because he loves*." Love always seeks to communicate. The lover longs to contact, to touch, the beloved — by a pressure of the hand, an intimacy, a word. There must be holy communion between Lover and loved, when the mind and heart and will of the One are disclosed to the other and a way is opened up for response. That is a matter of life and death.

Believing, then, in a God who speaks, and speaks because he loves, the Christian takes the next step and affirms that his God is a *God who sends*. The peak of this belief is reached in the Father's mission (sending) of the Son into the world that all may live through him. But this peak was reached through the comparative lowlands of preparatory sendings, and especially through that series of prophets through whom the word of the Lord, "at sundry times and in divers manners", came to men. It is extended into history through the members of Christ's body, the Church. "As my Father hath sent me, so send I you." The touch of the Father's love is felt in hospital and school, in inter-personal relationships, through word and sacrament. The mission continues unbroken and will do so while time endures. Preaching is concerned with that part of the divine mission which has to do with words, the communication of God's love, God's will, God's interest, to men and women in their need. There is an unbroken chain from the creative word of Genesis 1 to . . . to *you* as you preach next Sunday at St Agatha's.

Further, we Christians hold that the God who speaks, who loves, who sends, is also the *God who feeds*. A major part of a parent's life is concerned with the nourishment of the members of the family — whether the parent be the one who goes out to earn the money or the one who stays at home to prepare the food. Nourishment is literally vital. Within the household of God, it is the same. We have already noted the two focal points in a church building — the table round which the family gathers sacramentally to feed on Christ by faith with thanksgiving, and the pulpit where minds are stimulated, wills are touched, souls are nourished through the ministry of the Word. This is the ministry of edification, the building up of the Body of Christ. "When a man prophesies . . . his words have power to build;

they stimulate and they encourage . . . It is prophecy that builds up a Christian community" (1 Corinthians 14:3—4; N.E.B.).

So far, we have been engaging in *God-talk* (theology). That, we repeat, is the only starting point if we are serious in thinking about preaching.

We must now seek to enter into what the biblical writers meant when they spoke about a **word**. "What's in a word?", we say, and dismiss it with a wave of the hand. The Hebrew was not so foolish. To him a word was a thing of power. It got things done. If this is true in the sphere of human relationships, how much more true is it when God speaks. When God speaks, things happen — in the cosmos, in the history of nations, in the lives of men and women. The word is itself the deed.

Nowhere is this more powerfully put than in the creation story of Genesis 1. The writer paints a picture of primeval darkness. God spoke, and there was light. There was chaos. God spoke, and there was order, the separation of light from darkness, the splendid rhythm of evening and morning. A refrain runs through the drama of creation — "God said . . . " We watch the creative word at work. "He spake and it was done" (Psalm 33:9; cp.147:15ff.).

Genesis 1 is a seminal chapter. It lies behind the great prologue of John's Gospel. Here the word of Genesis is personalized. We must spell it with a capital W. *He*, present with God before creation began, was the Word through whom all things came to be. He was the life that was the light of men, a light which has never been mastered by the darkness, nor ever will be. That Word was enfleshed, and the glory of God was seen in the birth at Bethlehem. Grace and truth were there as man had never seen them before (v.14). There was an exposition of the mind and heart of God unique in its clarity and quality (v. 18).

The Genesis story of the creative word of God is seminal, too, in the thinking of Paul. In writing to the Corinthians (2 Corinthians 4:5—6), Paul puts his finger on "the light of revelation" as being the very heart of his preaching ("proclamation"). He can speak — he must speak — in terms of his own experience. There was darkness in the soul of Saul of Tarsus like the darkness spoken of in the Genesis story. God spoke: "Saul,

Saul, why . . . ?", the same God who said, "Out of darkness let light shine", and there was light. Chaos gave place to order. Saul, torn asunder by his pre-conversion conflicts, became a unity, a man in Christ.

The Genesis story is seminal, again, in the thinking of the unknown writer of the Epistle to the Hebrews. He has a preface which is in some ways similar to the preface to the Fourth Gospel. Here is the God who speaks, in "the Son . . . through whom he created all orders of existence". Others in former times had been the agents through whom, in fragmentary and varied fashion, God had spoken. "But in this final age he has spoken to us in the Son whom he has made heir to the whole universe . . . ."

Though Paul and the writer of the Epistle to the Hebrews never specifically speak of Jesus as "the Word", as John does, they get so close to that identification as to show clearly that their thinking is modelled on the Genesis story. There were other expressions open to John to use when he wrote about Jesus. He could have spoken of him as the Wisdom of God, for example, (there was a wealth of Wisdom literature on which he could have drawn to justify such a use). Or he could have spoken of him as the image of God (see, for example, Colossians 1:15 and cp. Hebrews 1:3). He fastened, however, on "the Word", because he wanted to shun anything which might suggest mere metaphysical speculation. In Jesus, God *spoke*. With him there is no disparity between word and deed. Jesus was God's mightiest act, in the sphere of human experience. Jesus not only *bore* the word of God to men, as the prophets had done. He *was*, himself, the Word. He was the peak-point in the Father's mission activity in the world.

When, earlier, we used the word "peak" of the Father''s revelation through the Son, we added: "The peak was reached through the comparative lowlands of preparatory sendings, and especially through that series of prophets through whom the word of the Lord . . . came to men." To those prophets we must now turn. It is not possible, in a book such as this, to undertake anything approaching a systematic examination of the Hebrew prophets, not even of those whose *writings* are found in the

Bible. But it would be foolish, in a book which deals with the ministry of the word of God, to bypass them. For they give us examples of men who believed, in their deepest beings and in spite of all that might seem to contradict that belief, in a God who speaks, who speaks because he loves, and who sends men as his spokesmen, for the fulfilling of his mission. "The message of the prophets . . . is like a lamp shining in a murky place, until the day breaks and the morning star rises to illuminate your minds" (2 Peter 1:19).

I propose, therefore, to look at four of these prophets in whose writings there is a disclosure of the nature of this God-prophet relationship, an unveiling of what it means to be a messenger of the Most High. What was it that enabled them to say: "Thus saith the Lord"? What theology, what religion, fashioned their preaching? How did they convey the picture of a God who, in *speaking* his mind, in *sending* his prophets, displayed his *love*, and *fed* his people? We shall look briefly at Amos, Hosea, Isaiah I, and Jeremiah.

AMOS

There is no record of Amos ever having had a blinding vision of the glory of God, as did Isaiah or, later, Saul of Tarsus. He is not one of the twice-born, if we interpret that phrase in the sense of sudden dramatic experience. The desert was God's secret training school in which he fashioned the character of this man. The desert seems to have been a favourite training place in the mind of God for those through whom he wished to speak with special clarity to his world. From Elijah, listening to "the sound of a gentle stillness" (1 Kings 19:12), to John Baptist to whom the people flocked in the wilderness (Matthew 3:5), to Jesus spending those formative forty days sent by the Spirit into the wilderness (Matthew 4:1), to the desert fathers whose tale has been memorably told by Helen Waddell, to Thomas Merton in our own day — so the story goes on.[1]

[1] I have elaborated this in my *Paul: Portrait of a Revolutionary*, chapter 3 (Hodder & Stoughton, 1984).

Amos, the load-carrier — his name derives from a root with that meaning; Amos, the man with a burden, and the burden no less than a word given him by the Almighty which he must off-load or break down; Amos, the eighth-century prophet, contemporary (roughly speaking) of Isaiah and Hosea — this man proved himself one of the greatest prophets. Alan Dunstan has defined the aim of the Hebrew prophets as follows: "(1) to expose the evil of the times, (2) to proclaim its consequences, (3) to recall people to the nature of their God, and (4) to call for a change of heart".[2] Amos well fulfils all these aims.

We do the prophets less than justice when we read their writings in little sections. Read Amos at a run, read it as if we had never read it before, and it will help us feel its full impact. It is rough, tough stuff.

Its harshness has in it something of the cruel winds and scorching sun of the desert. It denounces. It hurts. It stings. Amos is a kind of John Baptist in advance. If he has no "viper's brood" (Matthew 3:7), he has "you cows of Bashan" (4:1). I do not detect a sob in the throat of Amos, as there was in our Lord's when he cried out: "O Jerusalem, Jerusalem, the city that murders the prophets and stones the messengers sent to her! How often have I longed to gather your children, as a hen gathers her brood under her wings; but you would not let me"! (Matthew 23:37). If Amos knew how to weep for the sins of his people, there is little evidence of it in his prophecy. There is no softness, still less sentimentality in this book. But there is nobility.

The trouble was that there was softness among the people. Amos addresses his message to an affluent society, debilitated by luxury, surfeited with plenty. "You lie on beds of ivory, and sprawl upon your couches, eating choice lamb and farm-fed veal ... You ... drink wine by the bowl-ful and anoint yourselves with the finest oils" (6:4–6; J.B. Phillips). He excoriated the "cows of Bashan, women who glitter on the heights of Samaria, who defraud the poor, and ride roughshod over the needy, while you keep ordering your husbands, 'Bring us wine to drink' " (4:1).

[2] *Interpreting Worship*, p.37 (Mowbrays, 1984).

Meanwhile, as the rich get richer, the poor get poorer. The weak are trampled on, honest men browbeaten, poor men's claims for justice ignored (5:11—12). The needy are sold for the price of a pair of shoes, and shoddy business practices are pursued; sexual immorality abounds (2:6—8).

But do not complain that the people are irreligious! Oh no! They go on their religious pilgrimages; they bring their sacrifices; they sing their hymns (4:4—5 and 5:21—24). But it all stinks in the nostrils of Amos's God — "I loathe and despise your festivals . . . " (5:21). Religion without social justice is an abomination. "Let me have no more of your noisy hymns; my ears are closed to the music of your harps. Instead, let justice roll on like a mighty river, and integrity flow like a never-failing stream" (5:23—24).

Amos's God stood for social justice, for sincerity in religion; and therefore he was a God of judgement. There are inexorable consequences to wrong courses of action. God has a plumb-line in his hand (7:7—9). The day of the Lord is no phrase to tinker with; it is a prospect of darkness and disaster (5:18—20).

This message was tough not only on those upon whose backs the prophet's lashes fell, but on the prophet himself. To deliver a message of divine judgement and of wrath is to invite unpopularity. Amos got his ration in full.

George Adam Smith says that on the words of Amos's reply to Amaziah "we do not comment; we only do them homage". We recall the situation described in 7:10ff. Amaziah, "the Caiaphas of the Old Testament", had "informed" the king against Amos who dared to conspire against him in the very heart of Israel. To Amos he said: "This just isn't done — not in the capital. Run off and do your prophesying elsewhere. Try it out on the country bumpkins, not on the sophisticated townsmen." Amos's reply takes its place among the utterances of the immortals: "I was no prophet, nor was I a prophet's son. But the *Lord* took me, and the *Lord* said to me: 'Go, prophesy . . . '." There is a finality about such a reply which forbids any questioning. Amos had to obey, or abandon his prophetic task. He chose the former course, and remained true to the Lord.

So he remains within "the goodly fellowship of the prophets"

– not only with Hosea and Isaiah and Jeremiah, but with men like Micaiah, son of Imlah, who dared to give an unpopular answer to his monarch – "lock this fellow up and give him prison diet of bread and water" (1 Kings 22:1–28); and with Nathan, who dared to indict his sovereign with the blunt accusation "Thou art the man" (2 Samuel 12:1–14).[3]

HOSEA

If for Amos the desert was the place where the man was made and his message was determined, for Hosea it was not the desert but the home. For Hosea his home was a place of love – and of tragedy. Gomer deserted him and went off with another man. There was a child by their marriage and children by another man (for this seems the best interpretation of the opening verses of the prophecy which bears Hosea's name). And Hosea was left, broken-hearted.

The text of the book, as any Hebraist will admit, is difficult and dilapidated. This is due, no doubt, in part to scribal errors in its transmission. But its disorderliness reflects also the distress of the writer and a depth of passion too deep for orderly expression. The language is restless, irritable. Amazement, love, anger, anguish chase one another like clouds across the sky. The Jerusalem Bible describes Hosea as "a prophet at once affectionate and fiery".[4]

Years after Hosea's time, Paul was to speak of a "wound which is borne in God's way" and to contrast it with "the hurt which is borne in the world's way" (2 Corinthians 7:10). Hosea's wound was borne in God's way, but it was none the less deep for that. He brooded long and hard on the disaster which had hit him and his home. He loved Gomer with a love that was intense and true. (Does his hatred of the religious festivals reflect his experience of redeeming Gomer from one of the temples in

---

[3] In the quotations in this section, I have made considerable use of the translation-paraphrase of J.B. Phillips in his *Four Prophets* (Geoffrey Bles, 1963).
[4] p.1135 (1966 Edition).

which she had been a prostitute?) Heart-broken, he tried to make sense out of a nonsensical tragedy. Why had God allowed this to happen? There seemed to be no redeeming feature that he could see. And the names which God had bidden him to give to the children (*Lo-ruhamah*, "Not loved", or "She who has never known a father's pity", for the girl, and *Lo-ammi*, "Not my people", for the boy) only rubbed salt into the wound.

Then, very slowly, dimly at first and then a little more clearly, light began to dawn. Perhaps this tragedy was not wholly negative in its effect. Perhaps God might, in his wisdom, turn a minus into a plus (even if a plus is the sign of the cross). Perhaps out of this bad news of a broken marriage and a broken heart, the Good News of a Gospel might emerge. God loved Israel. And Israel had turned her back on God, and become a Gomer, had played the harlot, selling herself to be fertilized by others, by the *baalim*. Could it be that God's heart was broken, as Hosea's was? "Oh Ephraim, how shall I deal with you? How shall I deal with you, Judah? Your loyalty to me is like the morning mist, like dew that vanishes early" (6:4). "How can I give you up, Ephraim, how surrender you, Israel? How can I make you like Admah or treat you as Zeboyim?[5] My heart is changed within me, my remorse kindles already. I will not let loose my fury . . . " (11:8–9).

The language of married love predominates in this book. But imagery is piled on imagery, to paint as vividly as may be the picture of defection and of unrequited love. Israel is the unfaithful wife, but she is also the disobedient child — "When Israel was a boy, I loved him; I called my son out of Egypt; but the more I called, the further they went from me . . . It was I who taught Ephraim to walk, I who had taken them in my arms; but they did not know that I harnessed them in leading-strings and led them with bonds of love — that I have lifted them like a little child to my cheek, that I have bent to feed them" (11:1–4). Ephraim is a "cake half-baked" (7:8), "a silly senseless pigeon" (7:11), a nation whose political judgement is warped because moral judgement has gone by default. Decay has set into the very bones of the nation.

[5] Cities destroyed with Sodom and Gomorrah.

With God-given percipience Hosea puts his finger on the root of the trouble. "My people are ruined", he hears God say, "*for lack of knowledge*" (4:6), "there is no good faith or mutual trust, *no knowledge* of God in the land" (4:1). "Loyalty is my desire, not sacrifice, not whole-offerings but the *knowledge* of God" (6:6). And the word he uses for knowledge is the word that is frequently used of sexual intercourse – the marriage metaphor is pressed (and, we may add, reflected in Jeremiah, Ezekiel, Deutero-Isaiah, the Song of Songs and, supremely, in the New Testament). Priest and prophet alike are rebuked because they have been faithless in giving the knowledge of God to his people (chapter 4, etc.) – it is a terrible and searching indictment.

Hosea pleads with the people to repent. The word he uses can mean both *turn* and *return* (e.g. 2:7; 7:10; 14:2). The word has not got the subtlety of the Greek *metanoia*, which signifies a change of heart and mind resulting in a change in the way a person lives. But it is vivid enough. Turn back, it says. Come home. Turn round and face the facts of moral and political decay, of misery and guilt, of God's forgiveness and grace. Face the God from whom you have been running away and who

> "with unhurrying chase
> and unperturbèd pace,
> deliberate speed, majestic instancy"

has been eagerly seeking you.

What kind of God was Hosea's God? A God of judgement – yes. There is plenty of that in the book. But, above all else, a hurt God, a suffering God, a yearning God, a passionate God. It is not a very big step from Hosea's God to the Prodigal Father in the story of the two lost sons in Luke 15.

ISAIAH

Isaiah, though he was a contemporary of Amos, had a background entirely different from his. Isaiah was a man of the town, an aristocrat, who moved in court circles with ease. If we read chapters 37–39, virtually repeated in 2 Kings 18–20, we can see the intimacy of relationship which existed between King Hezekiah and the prophet – an intimacy, it may be noted, which did not hinder Isaiah from giving the king a warning (39:1–8), which showed a boldness comparable to that of Amos, or of Micaiah (1 Kings 22), or of Nathan (2 Samuel 12).

As we read through this collection of prophecies, we catch glimpses of the man, his prophetess wife, and two sons, Shear-jashub ("A remnant shall return", 7:3) and Maher-shalal-hash-baz ("speed-spoil-hasten-plunder", 8:1–4); we see the pressure of the Lord's hand on the prophet and hear the warning to honour and fear the Lord alone (8:11–15); we watch Isaiah underlining the urgency of his message by living barefoot and half-clad for three and a half years (20:1–6, almost after the enacted parabolic fashion of Jeremiah). The man emerges from the prophecies fitfully and partially. But it is in chapter 6 above any other place that we see the man face to face with his God, in an encounter which was to make him the man that he became – at the centre of affairs, his mind ranging out over surrounding nations, his political and international awareness always keen, his writings a strange mixture of judgement and mercy, of threats of punishment and passages of compassion.

"In the year of King Uzziah's death", i.e. 742 B.C. The phrase is far more than a note about a date in history. It points us to the story of the fall of a king who must have been something of an idol to the young prophet who grew up during his long and distinguished reign. The picture given of him in 2 Chronicles 26 is that of a monarch who lived up to the meaning of his name Uzziah, "Jehovah my strength". For fifty-two years he reigned, his rule marked by success in the field of battle and consolidation of the national life at home. "But when he grew powerful his pride led to his undoing: he offended against the Lord his God by entering the temple of the Lord to burn incense on the altar of incense" (v.16). Struck down with disease, he "remained a leper till the day of his death; he lived in his own house as a leper, relieved of all duties and excluded from the house of the Lord" (v.21).

It was in the year of the collapse and death of his king, Uzziah, that young Isaiah had the vision of another King, "high and exalted", the skirt of his robe filling the very temple which Uzziah had defiled. It was a moment at once of disillusionment, of disenchantment, and of vision, the latter being made the more vivid by the darkness of the former.

Language is strained in the attempt to express the majesty and holiness of God. The very seraphim hide their faces and their sexual parts ("feet", v.2, for, like Adam, they knew that they were naked) with their wings (v.2). "Holy, holy, holy is the Lord of Hosts", they cry. The temple shakes, and the smoke which fills it is perhaps not so much that of the customary incense as the mist which arises when holiness and sin come into contact one with the other.

The cry of the prophet, "Woe is me! I am lost . . . ", echoes the cry of the seraphim. He is a man of unclean lips, and he dwells among people of unclean lips. There can be no hand-shaking familiarity with God. For Isaiah, his consciousness of guilt centred in the mouth, in the *lips*. The mouth is the vent of the heart. The lips are the blossom of the man. "Out of the same mouth come praises and curses" (James 3:10). Isaiah feels the need of the cauterizing, cleansing fire which we men and women of the New Testament era know to be the touch of God's Spirit. With that touch comes not only cleansing — "See, this has touched your lips; your iniquity is removed, and your sin wiped away" (v.7) — but also commissioning — "Whom shall I send? Who will go for me?" (v.8).

The immediacy of forgiveness is no indication of cheap grace. There is no such thing — of that the cross of Christ is evidence. But when penitence is real, forgiveness is complete and the road is opened up for service.

There is a monosyllabic simplicity about the call — "Whom shall I send?" — and the response — "Here am I; send me." It reminds us of the response of Mary — "Here am I . . . as you have spoken, so be it" (Luke 1:38); and of the great assent of Jesus in the face of the cross — "Thy will be done" (Matthew 26:42).

Isaiah's God stands, as clearly as does the God of Amos, for social justice, for sincerity in religion — "No more shall you trample my courts. The offer of your gifts is useless, the reek of sacrifice is abhorrent to me" (1:12—13). And equally clearly he is a God of judgement. But Isaiah's special contribution — the thing that made him the man that he was and that moulded his message — was his concept of the holiness, the otherness of God: "Holy, holy, holy is the Lord of Hosts."

JEREMIAH

Young and diffident to the point of timidity, Jeremiah was nevertheless deeply convinced of the reality of his call from God — "Before I formed you in the womb I knew you for my own; before you were born I consecrated you, I appointed you a prophet to the nations" (1:5) — and of God's assurance of his presence with him and of his words put into his mouth (1:7—10). That assurance was to be tested again and again, but the experience recorded in the first chapter of the book must often have nerved and steadied him.

Celibate at the command of the Lord (16:1), he must have suffered from the lack of a home and family of his own. Misunderstood and persecuted by his own people, he came to realize "that they were hatching plots against me and saying, 'Let us cut down the tree while the sap is in it; let us destroy him out of the living, so that his very name shall be forgotten' " (11:19); " 'Come, let us invent some charges against him; let us pay no attention to his message' " (18:18). His arrest lay in the future (37:11ff.), as did his time in the muddy pit (chapter 38), and then in the guard house till Jerusalem fell (38:13ff.); but well before that he had cause to complain that "for twenty-three years . . . I have been receiving the words of the Lord and taking pains to speak to you, but you have not listened" (25:3). It was a long-drawn-out ordeal.

A man of intense sensitivity, he was tortured at the prospect, and later at the reality, of his people being deported. "How can I bear my sorrow? I am sick at heart. Hark, the cry of my people from a distant land: 'Is the Lord not in Zion? Is her King no longer there?' " (8:18—19). "On the pain of my wounds! Cruel are the blows I suffer. But this is my plight, I said, and I must endure it. My home is ruined, my tent-ropes all severed, my sons have left me and are gone, there is no one to pitch my tent again, no one to put up its curtains" (10:19–20).

All the time, he was conscious of the presence and activity of false prophets, men whose dastardly work was rewarded by the approval of an undiscerning people. "An appalling thing, an outrage, has appeared in this land: prophets prophesy lies and priests go hand-in-hand with them, and my people love to have it so. How will you fare at the end of it all?" (5:30–31). "All, high and low, are out for ill-gotten gain; prophets and priests are frauds, every one of them; they dress my people's wounds, but skin-deep only, with their saying, 'All is well'. All well? Nothing is well!" (8:10–11). "The shepherds of the people are mere brutes; they never consult the Lord, and so they do not prosper, and all their flocks at pasture are scattered" (10:21). The whole of chapter 23 is given over to a terrible indictment of false prophets, who buoy men up with false hopes and report a vision which comes from their own imagination and not from the mouth of the Lord.

Jeremiah's horror at this prostitution of prophecy was the greater because of his own sense of the weightiness of the prophetic office. To Jeremiah, a prophet was a *watchman* whose trumpet-call was to be obeyed (6:17); an *assayer* to test and try the people's conduct (6:27); a *shepherd* to tend and guard the sheep (10:21); a *burden-carrier*, in the sense of one to whom the word of the Lord is a burden to be carried and delivered (see especially the word-play in 23:33–40). Within him, Jeremiah experiences the word of the Lord as a scorching fire, a hammer that splinters rock (23:29; 20:9). Fire and hammer are powerful agents that get things done, realities with which a man trifles at his peril. "I will make my words a fire in your mouth; and it shall burn up this people like brushwood" (5:14).

So urgent to Jeremiah was the call to convey the word of God to the people that he sought means other than verbal to fulfil the task. Imagination should be the road to conscience. Eye-gate, the use of drama, should be used as well as ear-gate. Hence the series of extraordinary "enacted parables" which included those of the

44

rotting girdle (13:1—11), the shattered jar (19), the yoke which the prophet wore on his neck (27 and 28), the stones set in cement (43:8—13), the book thrown into the Euphrates (51:60—64). No doubt the people called him mad, an exhibitionist. But they could not rid their minds of the vivid visible symbols of prophetic truth which he used in his work.

The picture that is emerging is that of a tortured soul. It reminds us that there can be no prophecy without passion, no preaching without suffering. Nowhere is this seen more clearly than in those instances — and they are many — where we watch Jeremiah at prayer. Sometimes he cries out for vengeance (we recall that his were pre-Christian days) — "pour out thy fury on nations that have not acknowledged thee . . . " (10:25); "O Lord . . . I have committed my cause to thee; let me see thy vengeance upon them" (11:20), etc. But the real man of prayer is disclosed when we watch him arguing with God, in deep dialogue with God, even accusing God. "O Lord God, thou surely didst deceive this people and Jerusalem in saying 'You shall have peace', while the sword is at our throats" (4:10); and, more pointedly and personally, "O Lord, thou hast duped me, and I have been thy dupe; thou hast outwitted me and hast prevailed. I have been made a laughing-stock all the day long, everyone mocks me" (20:7). Sometimes he argues with God: "O Lord, I will dispute with thee, for thou art just" (12:1); "Must thou be like a man suddenly overcome, like a man powerless to save himself? Thou art in our midst, O Lord, and thou hast named us thine; do not forsake us" (14:9). Sometimes he pleads with God: "Thou knowest all that has passed my lips; it was approved by thee. Do not become a terror to me; thou art my only refuge on the day of disaster" (17:16b—17).

What does all this amount to? To us men of timid prayer and feeble preaching, some of this seems to verge on blasphemy. But it is nothing of the sort. Here in Jeremiah we have a man of utter reality, of openness in his dealings with God. And who dare say that God did not respect such religious honesty? Jeremiah was a suffering servant; and it was a fine tribute, if an unconscious one, when, on Christ's asking who men said he was, they answered, "Some say . . . Jeremiah" (Matthew 16:14).

If one asks of Jeremiah, of what kind was his relationship with God, it is not altogether easy to answer. Jeremiah approached God as one deeply conscious of a call and of God's promise of the help of his presence. The relationship of the man to God was close — there is indeed an element of intimacy about it. But it was stormy — with the storms of stark realism.

And if one asks what facets of God stand out above others which made Jeremiah the man and moulded his message, one must mention on the one hand the vivid concept of God as the God of history, concerned not only with Israel but with the nations which surrounded her, and on the other hand, the God of intimate relationships, the God of dialogue, the God who can be wrestled with.

*

In glancing thus briefly at four of the Old Testament prophets, we have been able to watch God at work in a peculiarly close relationship with the men through whom his word was to come to his people. The prophets have themselves to be made, re-made, fashioned anew, if they are to be agents of the God who speaks. The kind of men they were determined what they said and the power with which they said it. Their message resulted from the marriage of their theology with their own deep religion. That marriage generated a self-authenticating authority. Only so could they dare to say: "Thus says the Lord."

Almighty God,
who spoke to the prophets
that they might make your will and purpose known:
inspire the guardians of your truth,
that through the faithful witness of the few
the children of earth may be made one
    with the saints in glory;
by the power of Jesus Christ our Lord,
who alone redeemed mankind
and reigns with you and the Holy Spirit,
one God, now and for ever.

"The Word was made flesh and dwelt among us"

John 1:14

"Jesus came . . . preaching . . ."

Mark 1:14

3

The New Testament Background

JOHN THE BAPTIST AND JESUS

The age of the prophets seems to have been followed by a period of dreadful silence. There is a tragic note to this passage from Psalm 74:9 (thought by many to be a late Psalm of the Maccabaean era): "We cannot see what lies before us, we have no prophet now; we have no one who knows how long this is to last." The author of 1 Maccabees tells how, after the profanation of the temple in 168 B.C., Judas Maccabaeus arranged for the stones of the altar to be stored in a fitting place on the temple hill, "*until a prophet should arise* who could be consulted about them" (4:46). After the death of Judas, "it was a time of great affliction for Israel, worse than any since *the day when prophets ceased to appear among them*" (9:27). And the Jews and their priests confirmed Simon as their leader "until a true prophet should appear" (14:41). *The Song of the Three* laments: "We have no ruler, *no prophet*, no leader now" (v. 15).

Amos had spoken of a day to come when there would be a famine, not of bread or of water, but of hearing the word of the Lord (8:11–14). That is the ultimate in famine disaster, and the Jews had to endure its bitterness to the full.

But at last the silence was broken – by the coming of John the Baptist. His rough and rugged personality reminded his hearers of a former prophet, Elijah the Tishbite (2 Kings 1:8). His preaching told of a judgement-axe laid at the root of fruitless trees, of a winnowing fan separating chaff from wheat, of fire ready to destroy the worthless. His illustration of snakes fleeing before a forest fire and making for the nearest water struck home to the consciences of a crooked generation coming to him for baptism in the Jordan. When he spoke of the One who was to

51

follow him, he spoke in terms of fire and judgement — and flight (Matthew 3:7–12). But when Jesus came, his message was one of infinite tenderness. Not "flee", but "come". And John, hearing from prison reports of the words and acts of Christ, could only ask, incredulously: "Art thou he that should come, or look we for another?" (Luke 7:19–23). No wonder John was "scandalized"!

The heart of the Baptist's message, however, was positive. Not only "flee", but "repent, for the Reign of God is near". The word for repent, in the Aramaic which the Baptist used, was essentially simple — "turn round" or "return". *Turn round* and face the God from whom you have been running away; turn, and face his judgement, his grace, his forgiveness. *Return* to the God whom you have forsaken. Come home. That turning round, that returning was "with a view to the remission of sins" (Luke 3:3). The Baptist, whose "social Gospel" was pointed and direct (Luke 3: 10–14), put at the core of his message man's deepest need, forgiveness. A message which lacks that essential note is inadequate to meet our lostness.

The fearlessness of his preaching stands out. Whether he was addressing the common people (Luke 3:7ff.), or the religious leaders, the Pharisees and Sadducees who came to him for baptism (Matthew 3:7), or Herod the tetrarch of Galilee (Mark 6:17ff.), there was no trimming the sails of his message. In the words of the collect, he "constantly spoke the truth, boldly rebuked vice, and patiently suffered for the truth's sake". It cost him his life but, in this as in other ways, he prepared the way of the Lord whose fearless ministry was to lead him to the cross.

The picture which the Fourth Gospel gives of the Baptist differs in many ways from that of the Synoptists, or, perhaps we should say, fills it out considerably. It makes much of his work as a witness (John 1:7), as a "voice of one crying . . . " (1:23) with an urgency born of deep conviction; as the "best man" of the Bridegroom (3:29); as a "lamp that blazed and shone" (5:35), "decreasing" even to the point of guttering out in death, in order that Christ might "increase" (3:30) and be seen to be the Light of the world.

Rugged, fearless, fiery, loyal to the point of self-immolation,

John Baptist broke the silence, and the prophetic task of preaching began again.

Jesus took up the torch which John had dropped. We have already touched on the subject of Jesus as the Word of God, the Word incarnate, enfleshed. Like the prophets, he bore the word of God to men. Unlike them, Jesus *was* the Word of God. Therein lies his uniqueness. But we must ask this question: If we had been among the crowds who listened to Jesus as he preached in Galilee or in the temple courts at Jerusalem, what impressions should we have gained? What would have been the marks of his preaching which would have registered on us most forcefully and compelled us to say, "Never man spoke like this man" (John 7:46), and that made crowds hang on his words so closely that they forgot the demands of physical hunger (Matthew 14:13ff.)? We may mention some which stand out clearly.

There was a **winsomeness**, a personal charm about this preacher. When John says that he "dwelt among us full of *grace* and truth" (1:14), he uses a word (*charis*) which sometimes means simply graciousness. No doubt there is much more to the word as it is used in this passage, but at least it includes the idea of winsome attractiveness. It is interesting that, when Luke is recording the reaction of the synagogue congregation to Jesus" first sermon in his home-town after his baptism, he mentions that the hearers were astonished that words of such grace should fall from his lips (4:22). They had never thought of religion quite like that – it was a lovely thing as he painted it. Does John echo this note when he describes Jesus the Good Shepherd not in terms of moral goodness (*agathos*) but of beauty (*kalos*, 10:11)?

There was a **simplicity** about this man's preaching, a simplicity in the language he used. In this respect, we may contrast it with the language used by the apostle Paul. Paul was a town man, an academic. Jesus was a country man and his contemporaries called him "untrained" (John 7:15). That, no doubt, accounts in part for the differences between Master and apostle; in part, but not wholly.

Simplicity of language is often the mark of a great teacher. He has so wrestled with the profundities of thought that he can reduce them to simple language without evacuating them of their content. Bishop Stephen Neill used to say that if, when he had written a sentence, he found that it was impossible to translate it easily into another language, there was something wrong with the sentence. There is also a simplicity which is the mark of a simpleton. But the real simplicity is the mark of one who has so travailed with an idea, a concept, that he can break it down into a language "understanded of the people".

Tyrrell Green says of our Lord:

> He spoke of lilies, vines and corn,
> The sparrow and the raven;
> And words so natural yet so wise
> Were on men's hearts engraven.
> And yeast and bread and flax and cloth
> And eggs and fish and candles —
> See how the most familiar world
> He most divinely handles.

There was an **authority** about the preaching of Jesus which was self-authenticating. This was at once noticed by the people. It marked the teaching as different from that of the other teachers of the day (Mark 1:22). "Rabbi A in the name of Rabbi B says this. But Rabbi C in the name of Rabbi D says the other" — so their teaching ran. But this teacher said: "*I* say to you . . ." (Matthew 5:22, 28, 32, 34, 39, 44). And that was that. Perhaps this authority arose, at least in part, from our Lord's self-identification with the people to whom he preached. True, in one sense, he was "separate from sinners" (Hebrews 7:26). But in another sense, he stood in with them. At his baptism, he did so ("*We* do well to conform . . ." Matthew 3:15). As the people watched him going about his healing work, they recalled the words of Isaiah (53:4): "He took away our illnesses and lifted our diseases from us" (Matthew 8:17). He invited them to share a yoke with him — they would find it easy: it would not irk (Matthew 11:29–30). Men had to listen when he spoke like that. There was authority behind his words, the authority of self-authenticating holiness. When he called, they obeyed (Mark 1:18).

There was an **urgency** about the preaching of Jesus. There was no note of "take it or leave it". The preaching ministry of Jesus began "after John was put in prison" (Mark 1:14). The work had to be carried on. No state tyranny must be allowed to interfere with the proclamation of the word of God. If John the Baptist is forced to drop the torch, Jesus will pick it up.

The friends of Jesus tell him of crowds waiting for him. He replies that he and his disciples must push on to the next towns "that I may preach there also; for to this end came I forth" (Mark 1:38). There was an urgent mission to be fulfilled. A study of the word "must" in the Fourth Gospel — a word which, as Hoskyns says, "denotes a divine requirement" — only underlines this sense of urgency (see John 3:7, 14; 4:20, 24; 9:4; 10:16; 12:34; 20:9).

If the source of this urgency be sought, it is to be found in our Lord's deep interest in and concern for people. People mattered. They mattered because they were made to be sons and daughters of the Father-God. The image in which they were made had been marred. He must restore it. It was to him a positive passion, and from that passion the power of his preaching stemmed.

There was a **positive directness** about the preaching of Jesus. Hence his avoidance of the abstract. He does not say "Benefi-cence should be unostentatious". He says: "When you do some act of charity, do not announce it with a flourish of trumpets" (Matthew 6:2). Hence his constant use of parables, brilliant little stories, calling for a laugh or a nod of agreement or a protest, but aimed at conscience and will, aimed at decision and a verdict. No long application is needed at the end of the parable. Leave it as it is: it will do its own incisive work. The parable of the rich fool (Luke 12:16–21), so briefly and so vividly told, cuts like a knife — where is *my* wealth? So also the parable of the Pharisee and the tax-gatherer (Luke 18:9–14) — do I pray, or do I patter? In what do I trust when my standing with God is at stake? No wonder that John in his Gospel makes *crisis* one of his major themes — there is inevitably an element of divisiveness when Jesus speaks — the hearer stands at the point of a great divide and he alone can decide which road he takes. Here again, Jesus proves himself to be in the prophetic succession.

The preaching of Jesus **respected the intelligence of his hearers**. It was addressed to the adult mind. By this I do not mean that a child is unable to understand the teaching of Jesus. Sometimes he is better at this than is the grown-up, cluttered as the latter is with riches and worldly cares (Mark 4:19). What I mean is that Jesus refused to treat people like children who have constantly to be given specific instructions, clear directions on specific points of conduct. He relied on their capacity to think and to decide. Often he seems to have refused to give a straight answer to a straight question. If they asked him "Who is my neighbour?", he would tell them a story and they must work it out (Luke 10:29ff.). If a man asked him to speak to his brother and tell him to be fair, he would answer "Who set me over you to judge or arbitrate?" (Luke 12:14). "He that has ears to hear let him hear." He who has brains and a conscience, let him use them. Tough? He was. He will show the direction, rather than give directions: "This is the way: walk in it." It is on the way, as men walk, that they will find the truth. This is teaching with the sharp tang of fresh air about it. It braces. It makes demands.

Winsomeness, simplicity, authority, urgency, directness, respect for the intelligence of his hearers — if these were among the marks which distinguished the preaching of Jesus, no wonder that people listened! These, and an honesty which was transparent, could not fail to make a deep impression on mind and conscience. But there was more, far more, to the preaching of Jesus than outward marks. Its most potent factor was its **content**. This it was which gave it its enormous thrust; and to this we must turn, however briefly.

His preaching was essentially **God-centred**. His sermons could never be accused of being talks on contemporary philosophy, politics or economics with a dash of religion thrown in. His main theme, to which he returned again and again, was the Reign of God in this world and the next, in society and in the individual. The prophets and the psalmists had had much to say about God's Reign, but when Jesus took up the subject he struck a new note and gave the theme a new content. "In his hands the thing became a trumpet." God's Reign was not something simply to be anticipated with hope or fear. It had arrived. It was "upon you", the hearers, as Mark puts it (1:15). And it had arrived in the Person of the preacher. Because Jesus was standing there, heralding the arrival of the Reign, an entirely new situation was opening up. God reigns, and the earth may be glad thereof!

If we may put it in terms of grammar, the preaching of Jesus was in the *indicative* mood. He does not begin with an imperative, or make a demand on his hearers. He announces a joyful fact — God reigns! And if we may put it in terms of music, the theme is announced in the major key: Joy to the world, the Lord has come and visited his people! The finger of God is at work, with power; devils are being driven out; the Kingdom of God has arrived (Luke 11:20).

Of course, the indicative is followed by the imperative — "Repent, and believe the Gospel". But even the word "repent", as it falls from the lips of Jesus, has about it a ring of joy. For what happens when a man repents? He turns round. And what, or rather whom, does he find as he turns? He finds God who, in his love, has been following him all the time, the Hound of Heaven who will not let him go. To come face to face with such a God, the source of all joy, is an exhilarating experience. "Repent, and believe the Gospel." To grasp the good news and to enter into its implications is to discover new sources of life and power. The imperatives ("Repent, and believe the Gospel") which follow the great indicative ("God's Reign is upon you") are not a list of dreary negatives ("thou shalt not . . . "). They are pointers to the only way to live life as God intends his children to live it.[1]

The figures of speech which Jesus used in his preaching indicate the arrival in his person of powers hitherto only dimly glimpsed. What duller substance is there than dough? But allow some yeast to get to work in it, and things begin to move, for yeast is full of life (and vitamin B, as we should say) (Matthew 13:33). Water is good, even life-giving, but it is poor stuff for a joyful wedding feast. New wine and plenty of it — this is what the preacher from Galilee talks about and provides (with Matthew 9:17 cp. John 2:1–11). Exuberance, like wine that makes glad the heart of man (Psalm 104:15), accompanies the

---

[1] On this, see further chapter 7.

presence of the Man they designated as a wine-bibber (Matthew 11:19)! People are beset by forces too strong for them; but Jesus has come to grips with these forces, has invaded Satan's territory and tied up the tyrant (Matthew 12:29). True, the final day of man's emancipation lies in the future; but a bridgehead into enemy territory has been made, a new order has been initiated, and things can never be the same again.

The result of such preaching is seen in a certain carefreeness which marks the men and women of the Reign. There is no need for anxiety; indeed, it is forbidden, for the King is also the Father (Matthew 6:25ff.). This King looks for loyalty and obedience, this Father for a response of love. Given that, all the treasuries of heaven are open and available. The distinctive cry of Jesus seems to have been "Fear not. Be of good cheer".

This is not to say that God's children are encouraged to withdraw from the troubles of this world into a passive anticipation of a coming Utopia. Far from it. One of the marks of these men and women is precisely their implication in the world's needs and griefs. The Good Samaritan is called good just because he is the first on the scene of the disaster who does anything practical for the thug's victim (Luke 10:30ff.). If we are to have the Father's blessing, we must have dealings with the hungry, the thirsty, the homeless, the ill-clad, the sick, the prisoners (Matthew 25:31ff.). The men and women of the Reign are very earthy folk, their hands are dirty and calloused, because they are followers of the incarnate and crucified Lord. Taking up the cross and following the Christ draws blood.

THE ACTS OF THE APOSTLES

When we turn from the gospels, from the preaching of John Baptist and of our Lord, to the preaching of the early Church, we are dependent almost entirely on the Acts of the Apostles, apart from the evidence of Paul's letters (which we shall examine separately). It is not easy to assess the evidence of the Acts, for many of the discourses recorded in that book are not sermons as we understand that word. Many of those discourses are, naturally, resumés. Many of them, no doubt, bear marks of Lucan "editing". And, again, many of them are replies to immediate situations, for example, of arrest by the authorities, rather than expositions of Christian truth, though even in such addresses certain basic convictions shine through as being central to the speakers" faith.

The two main speakers are, of course, Peter and Paul. In the case of **Peter**, the most outstanding feature of his utterances, as given to us in the Acts, is the centrality of the person of Jesus. This dominates the whole scene. It shines through what he says in a variety of situations with the brilliance of a newly discovered truth. It reflects a kind of awed surprise at the power of the "name" of the man from Nazareth. Thus, on the day of Pentecost (2:14ff.) he faced the bewildered multi-racial crowd, and swiftly dealt (not without a touch of humour − "it is only nine in the morning") with the suggestion that the people were the worse for drink! He saw in the events of that day a fulfilment of what the prophet Joel had anticipated − a pouring out upon everyone of the Spirit of God. Then, without further ado, he comes to the point: "Listen to me: I speak of Jesus of Nazareth" (v.22).

Again, after the healing of the cripple at the gate of the temple, Peter addresses the astonished crowd. He had scarcely opened his mouth before he focused the attention of his hearers on God's "servant Jesus . . . whom God . . . raised from the dead . . . " And the name of Jesus . . . has strengthened this man (3:13−16). "When God raised up his Servant, he sent him to you first . . . " (v. 26). He gave a similar answer to the religious leaders, scandalized as they were by such an act of healing at the hands of such "unprofessional" men. "If . . . we are asked by what means he was cured, here is the answer . . . : it was by the name of Jesus Christ of Nazareth, whom you crucified, whom God raised from the dead" (4:5ff.).

When the apostles were arrested and brought before the Council, Peter replied to the examining High Priest: "We must obey God rather than men", and at once proceeded to speak of the crucified and risen Lord (5:29ff.). His reply to the enquiring Cornelius again went straight to the point −"the good news of peace through Jesus Christ . . . Jesus of Nazareth . . . anointed with the Holy Spirit . . . doing good and healing . . . put to death by hanging on a gibbet . . . raised to life on the third day . . . " (10:34ff.). Again and again, his answers, his "preaching", came back to the person of Jesus, as the needle of a compass swings to the magnetic north.

If we were to summarize the two main emphases which recur in the preaching of Peter, they would be: (i) the conviction that what they had seen in their recent companionship with Jesus and in the after-events of Pentecost was a "fulfilling" of what the ancient Scriptures had said, and (ii) the concentration on the person of Jesus as the one through whom God had been and was continuing to be uniquely at work.

In the case of **Paul**, much of what is recorded of his speeches had to do with such matters as the Council of Jerusalem (chapter 15) and his *apologiae* before Felix (chapter 24) and Agrippa (chapter 26), not with ordinary preaching material. But as in the case of Peter, so also of Paul, we find the same emphasis on the fulfilment of Scripture when he was addressing fellow Jews (13:27 and 32ff.). And here, again like Peter, he "homes in" on the person of Jesus as the centre of "the message of this salvation", the one on "the gibbet . . . laid in a tomb . . . raised from the dead" (26ff.). Even when he addressed a predominantly Gentile audience on Mars Hill in Athens, where reference to the fulfilment of Scripture would have been meaningless and references to their own poets were more apposite, he could not conclude his address without a powerful reference to the "man of [God's] choosing", raised from the dead (17:22–31). Bidding farewell to the elders of the church gathered at Miletus, Paul summarized the essence of his message as "repentance before God and trust in our Lord Jesus" (20:21) and the proclamation of "the Kingdom" (v.25). Back in Jerusalem, making his defence and telling the story of his conversion, it was his personal encounter with Jesus of Nazareth on which he laid stress, the Lord who said "Saul, Saul, why do you persecute me?" (22:1–21). (Was this the beginning of his belief in the Church as the Body of Christ?) It was the same when he made his defence before Agrippa (26:2ff.).

The addresses of both Peter and Paul reflect the atmosphere of the early Church as it is depicted in the Acts — an atmosphere of surprised delight at the privilege of being in on God's activity in the person of his Son; of the joy of discovery ("*this* is that of which the Scriptures spoke"): a sense that powers unrealized before were operative in their midst; a sense of boldness and of responsibility.

If the emphasis on the earthly life and ministry of Jesus surprises us by its slightness — the Acts adds nothing to our knowledge of the Jesus of the gospels except the valuable saying, "Happiness lies more in giving than in receiving" (20:35) — the emphasis on the death and resurrection of Christ is constant and forceful. The early Church saw in it the hand of God (2:23; 4:28) and the clue to the redemption of sinners. They never mention the cross alone; the crucified is always the risen and exalted, the destined judge and saviour. Equally frequent in the preaching is the emphasis on repentance. This it was which gave preaching its objective, for repentance is the reorientation of a man or woman in relation to God and his purposes, the beginning of a life-long pilgrimage from the mind of the flesh to the mind of Christ.

In the Acts, there are four *main* words used for the activity of Christian preaching.

(a) The first is *euangelizomai*, the word which we have transliterated as *evangelize* and which means "to announce good news". This occurs ten times, and in nine of those ten occurrences the content of the preaching is described. (The other passage is 8:40 — "he evangelized all the cities".) In four of these nine passages, the object is either simply "Jesus" (8:35), or "Jesus Christ" (5:42), or "the Lord Jesus" (11:20), or "Jesus and the resurrection" (17:18). In two passages, the object is "the Word" (8:4) or "the word of the Lord" (15:35). In the remaining three passages interesting hints are given as to the prevailing emphasis of the message: "concerning the Reign of God and the Person of Jesus Christ" (8:12), "peace through Jesus Christ" (10:36), and "that you should turn from these vanities to the living God" (14:15). (See also pp. 66–67.)

(b) The second word is *katangello*, which means "to announce" or "publish". It occurs six times, once with the simple object

"Jesus" (17:3 — "that He is the Christ"), once with its subject (17:13), and twice with its object (13:5; 15:36) "the word of God" or "the word of the Lord", once with the object "the resurrection of the dead" — "the resurrection of Jesus" (4:2) and once with the subject "the forgiveness of sins" (13:38).

(c) The third word is *kerusso*, which means "to herald". This occurs eight times, of which only five are relevant to our purpose. (Of the other three, one has no object (10:42), one refers to the preaching of John the Baptist (10:37), and one refers to the preaching which found its centre in Moses (15:21).) Three of these five have as their object the simple words "the Christ" (8.5), or "Jesus, that He is the Son of God" (9:20), or "Jesus" (19:13), while the remaining two have "the Reign" (20:25) and "the Reign of God" (28:31).

(d) The last word is *laleo*, the simplest of the four words. It is used frequently in the straightforward sense of "speaking" or "talking", and is itself suggestive of the informality of the early Christian preaching. One occurrence (13:42) throws no light on our question. In all the other four passages the object is "the word" or "the word of the Lord" — (8:25; 11:19; 14:25; 16:6).

What results may we glean from our work on the Acts of the Apostles? The findings are easy to gather, for we have but to look over the instances cited above.

(i) Perhaps the favourite way of summarizing the content of the preaching was in the pregnant phrase "*the word* (of the Lord, of God)", that is to say, not only a word *about* God, but the word which comes *from* God. Here is the prophetic note of the Old Testament enriched with all the wealth of the great central events of the life and death and resurrection of Christ.

(ii) An almost equally popular way of stating the object of the preaching was to give the name "Jesus", sometimes elaborated as "Jesus Christ", or "Jesus, the Son of God". This is as remarkable for its simplicity as for its profundity. The centre alike of the preaching and of the living of the early Church was the Person of their Risen Lord. Bishop F. R. Barry expressed it well: "The good news that thundered across the Roman Empire and brought back hope to a disillusioned world was not prescriptions about Christian conduct: it was "Jesus and the Resurrection". It went out with a victory behind it."[2]

Now the connection between these two groups of objects is very close. For no early Christian preacher could preach "the word" without preaching "Jesus Christ", nor, conversely, could he preach "Jesus Christ" without preaching "the word of God". So we may come to the conclusion that, in the Acts of the Apostles, we have an approximation to that great doctrine which we associate with the Fourth Evangelist, and which we call the doctrine of the Logos. *He* is the focal centre of the early Christian preaching. Apart from him, the Church has nothing to proclaim. "Jesus Christ our Lord − this", says Karl Barth, "is the Gospel and the meaning of history."[3]

(iii) The third group of objects may be regarded as elaborations or outcomes of the first two. Thus, when the early Christians preached "the Reign of God", they did so because in Christ that Reign had received a unique embodiment, and had, indeed, been the core of his own teaching. Again, when they preached "peace by Jesus Christ" or "the forgiveness of sins", they looked back to Bethlehem and Calvary, to the great historic events where God in Christ had "visited and redeemed his people".

There are other words used in the Acts in connection with the theme of conveying the word of God to men. But the four which we have mentioned are sufficient for our purpose here, and we shall have more to say about three of them when we come to the Pauline letters, to which we now turn.

PAUL

In turning to the Pauline material, we cannot, of course, regard Paul's letters as sermons. They are precisely what they purport to be − letters occasioned by local situations in the young churches which called for direction, advice, comment, rebuke. Even Romans, the most weighty of the letters, is a careful statement (of which a kind of outline had been given in Galatians) called forth by a particular pastoral-doctrinal issue which Paul saw to be of

[2] *Faith in Dark Ages*, pp. 60−61.
[3] *Epistle to the Romans*, p. 29, English translation, 1933.

far more than local importance; indeed he believed that the future of the Church depended on a right approach to it.

He was anxious to make it clear that in no way did he distort the original message of the Church (2 Corinthians 4:2, cp. 2:17). He had received that message, presumably from the early disciples at Damascus at the time of his conversion, and had handed on what he had received. He regarded himself as a trustee — committed to elaborate indeed, but not to manipulate. That message, as he described it in 1 Corinthians 15:3ff., had about it those same marks which we noticed in the Acts of the Apostles — it centred on the person of Christ, and more particularly on the events of Good Friday and Easter Day. "I handed on to you the facts which had been imparted to me: that Christ died for our sins, in accordance with the Scriptures; that he was buried; that he was raised to life on the third day, according to the Scriptures; and that he appeared to Cephas, and afterwards to the Twelve . . . " Indeed, in relation to the Eucharist he claimed, in the same letter (11:23), that what he had received from the Lord he handed on to the Corinthians, and he commended them (11:2) for maintaining those traditions. The early tradition mattered. It was a sacred thing to be carefully guarded. His life-work was to communicate it.

The language which he used about preaching and teaching sheds a clear light on how he regarded this task of communication, and is deserving of careful study. Here we touch on a variety of words of primary importance:

(i) The word *kerusso*, generally but not always translated *proclaim* in the New English Bible, is connected with the idea of heralding. A herald, according to Grimm-Thayer's New Testament lexicon, is described as one "vested with public authority, who conveyed the official messages of kings, magistrates, princes, military commanders, or who gave a public summons or demand, and performed various other duties". We note that he was invested with an authority other than his own; that he conveyed the message of his sovereign; and he looked for a response of obedience from those who heard him. In the Graeco-Roman world, the office of such men was a sacred one and their persons were inviolable, being under the immediate protection of the god who sent them. Plato, in *The Laws* (p.941), stressed the solemn responsibility of the herald: "If a herald or an ambassador carry a false message from one city to another, or bring back a false message from the city to which he is sent, or be proved to have brought back, whether from friends or enemies, in his capacity of herald or ambassador, what they have never said, let him be indicted for having violated, contrary to the law, the commands and duties imposed upon him by Hermes or Zeus, and let there be a penalty fixed, which he shall suffer or pay, if he be convicted."

Paul must have been well aware of these things when he used the word in connection with his preaching work. The most significant passage in his writings about this is in his second letter to the Corinthians (4:5−6): "It is not ourselves that we proclaim; we proclaim Christ Jesus as Lord, and ourselves as your servants, for Jesus' sake." If his hearers asked him why this should be so, he is quick with his answer. It is because "the same God who said, 'Out of darkness let light shine', has caused his light to shine within us, to give the light of revelation − the revelation of the glory of God in the face of Jesus Christ." It was because he had been at the receiving end of a revelation that he could, and must, preach. It was as if another creation had taken place in his own person, a creation comparable with that recorded in the first chapter of Genesis when, in response to the divine word, light shone out of darkness, order emerged from chaos. That revelation, that experience of new creation in Christ, must be shared by proclamation, and the herald (for all his authority) will do it as their "slave for Jesus' sake".

(ii) The idea of *ambassadorship* is close to that of being a herald, though the occurrence of the former is much less frequent in Paul's letters than is that of the latter. But the two passages where it does occur must not pass unnoticed. "We come . . . as Christ's ambassadors. It is as if God were appealing to you through us: in Christ's name, we implore you, be reconciled to God!" (2 Corinthians 5:20). And again: "Pray for me, that I . . . may boldly and freely make known his hidden purpose, for which I am an ambassador − in chains" (Ephesians 6:19−20). The idea of a manacled ambassador has about it a touch of wry humour!

Again we catch the note of delegated authority — an ambassador comes not in his own name but as representative of his sovereign. His office is one of great delicacy, for his master will be judged by the character as well as by the words of the man who has been sent to the country concerned. Martin Luther, in his *Commentary on St Paul's Epistle to the Galatians*, makes the point well: "An ambassador speaks not of himself, or as a private person, but for his king, and in his king's name. As representing the king he is honoured and set in a place he would not occupy as a private person. Wherefore, let the preacher of the Gospel be certain that his calling is from God."

Those who know anything of the art of diplomacy know how many and how searching are the demands made on the character of the diplomat. "Diplomacy" has about it the ring of tact and skill. An ambassador lacking in intelligence or in loyalty to his sovereign or in courtesy in his dealings with those to whom he was sent, would soon be withdrawn from the service. He must be something of an expert in the art of interpretation, putting into the language of the people the will and desires of the sovereign whom he represents. What he stands for can easily be misunderstood, and the consequences of such misunderstanding can be serious, even leading on occasion to war.

(iii) The idea behind such words as *evangel*, and *evangelist* is of frequent occurrence in the New Testament (see p. 61). Indeed, the verb occurs in classical Greek as well as in the Greek translation of the Old Testament (the Septuagïnt). For example, Isaiah exclaimed: "How lovely on the mountains are the feet of the herald who comes to . . . *bring good news*, the news of salvation" (52:7). In the passage quoted by our Lord in the Nazareth synagogue, Isaiah had written: "The spirit of the Lord God is upon me because the Lord . . . has sent me to *bring good news* to the humble . . . " (61:1). In the New Testament the meaning of the good news is infinitely deepened and enriched by the events of Bethlehem, Calvary and Pentecost. Paul looked back on the mighty acts of God in Christ. He had "visited and redeemed his people", and Paul had to exclaim: "O depth of wealth, wisdom, and knowledge in God! How unsearchable his judgements, how untraceable his ways!" (Romans 11:33). The rescue of the people from Egypt was but a dim foreshadowing of the redemption wrought by Christ. This was the central core of the evangel with the proclamation of which he was entrusted. One day he would stand before "the tribunal of Christ" (2 Corinthians 5:10) and give an account of his discharge of his work as a good-news man.

(iv) The next two words may be taken together. The first is *dialegomai*, which we recognise in the word *dialogue*. It means "to discuss, argue, reason with". It is not used *by* Paul in his letters but it is used six times in the Acts *about* his work as a communicator of the Gospel. A vivid instance is in 17:2–3: "For the next three Sabbaths he argued with them, quoting texts of Scripture which he expounded and applied to show that the Messiah had to suffer and rise from the dead. 'And this Jesus', he said, 'whom I am proclaiming to you, is the Messiah'." We can hear the sound of heated debate, of thrust and counter-thrust, of elucidation, of persuasion. Which leads us to the second and somewhat similar word, *peitho*, "to prevail upon, to persuade, to win over". This word again is used some six times about Paul's work, suggesting that he was not content merely to win an intellectual victory or to score points in a debate. He sought conviction; he looked for the registering of a decision which affected conduct as well as mind, which influenced the whole man. Such persuasion was not proselytism – that word suggests pressurizing. Paul's "prevailing" went far deeper – to the roots of human personality. (Paul himself uses the verb, about his work, in Galatians 1:10, and the adjective "persuasive" in 1 Corinthians 2:4.)

Herald, ambassador, evangelist, persuader – these words all give, as it were, slanting rays of light on the nature of Paul's communication of the Gospel, as he saw that task. But behind them lay two other concepts, perhaps more basic than any of the words which we have so far considered. They were the words "apostle" and "slave".

(v) **Apostle**. Paul might say, and with deepest sincerity, that he was not fit to be called an apostle (1 Corinthians 15:9). He could never forget the days when he had persecuted the Church. None the less, he constantly used the word, with great emphasis – he *was* "an apostle, not by human appointment or human commission, but by commission from Jesus Christ and from God the Father" (Galatians 1:1) — and sometimes with a measure of sharpness when he was faced by those who decried or questioned his authority — "Am I not a freeman? Am I not an apostle? Did I not see Jesus our Lord?" (1 Corinthians 9:1); "In no respect did I fall short of these superlative apostles, even if I am a nobody. The marks of a true apostle were there, in the work I did among you . . . " (2 Corinthians 12:11–12). Above all else, it was the experience on the Damascus road that convinced him of his mission and of his position as an apostle: "I have appeared to you for a purpose: to appoint you my servant and witness . . . I will rescue you from this people and from the Gentiles to whom I am *sending* you" (Acts 26:16–17). The verb is that from which the word *apostle* derives. He was, as he stated at the beginning of his letter to the Romans, an "apostle by God's call, set apart for the service of the Gospel" (1:1). If the risen Christ had appeared to the Ten and said to them, "As the Father sent me, so I send you" (John 20:21), he had as certainly sent Paul, and the note of apostleship is sounded in practically every letter of his which is ours to read. The basic reason for Paul's opposing Peter to his face was that the latter had "turned his apostleship upside down and played the Pharisee" (T.W. Manson's paraphrase of Galatians 2:12), and no man dare thus treat God's call.

(vi) **Slave**. There is a note of authority, even of status, about the word "apostle". There is no such note about the word "slave" — not at least in the world's usage. There is nothing lower in the world's vocabulary than *doulos*. A slave has no rights of his own. He belongs body and soul to his master — he is part of his property. Indeed he may well bear on his body the *stigmata* which mark him out as this man's slave, and not that man's. And yet — here is the great Pauline paradox of vocabulary and of experience — this word *doulos* is as dear to him as the word *apostolos*: *slave* and *apostle* can stand together in a kind of holy juxtaposition. "Paul, slave of Christ Jesus, apostle by God's call . . . " (Romans 1:1). It was in that servanthood that he had found his freedom, and he gloried in it.

The idea of a man as a servant of God has a fine biblical

ancestry. The great "Servant Songs" of Isaiah (42:1ff.; 49:1ff.; 50:4–11; 52:13–53:12) were surely basic to our Lord's concept of his own ministry — he was determined not to exercise the use of force but of love, "not to be ministered unto but to minister", and to take upon himself the marks of willing slavery which had been adumbrated in Isaiah's prophecies. What more fitting course could there be than that Paul should tread in his steps and, suffering for him the loss of all things, assume as his Master did the form of a slave?

Apostle and slave; authority and servanthood. The elevation of the pulpit in the furnishing of a church "is not in order to indicate the elevation of the preacher's person: it is raised aloft to indicate the majesty of that event upon which preacher and congregation together wait, namely, Christ's presence and speaking through the written testimony of prophets and apostles. . . . . Alas for the hapless preacher who imagines that it is raised high in order to be a platform for the exhibition of his learning, eloquence, humour and impressive personality, forgetting that it is the throne of Jesus Christ from which he alone is to rule his people."[4]

Almighty God,
who gave to your apostles
grace truly to believe and to preach your word:
grant that your Church
may love that word which they believed
and may faithfully preach and receive the same;
through Jesus Christ our Lord.

A Note to the Reader

The purpose of the foregoing chapters on the biblical background of preaching is a practical one. It might, therefore, be of help to postpone going further in the reading of this book at this stage, and to glance back over the material already covered, asking certain questions. For example:

Granted that the circumstances which faced the prophets, John the Baptist and Jesus, Peter and Paul, were very different from those which face us in the late twentieth century, what was there in their preaching which is timeless? What are the main truths — about God, man, human destiny, ethics — which are pertinent at all periods of history? Can we sift the permanent from the passing — in the content of the preaching, in its aim, in the manner of its presentation? (We may instance one matter where their emphasis and ours are likely to be very different: The New Testament preachers made much of the method of "proving" recent events by reference to Old Testament texts — "this is that which was spoken by . . . ". That method is hardly likely to be profitable in a world whose people are largely ignorant of the contents of the Old Testament and of how to handle them.)

The discipline of asking such questions, of writing down our findings, and then of comparing our preaching with that of the biblical preachers will be of benefit. The comparison may be a revelation of our own nakedness. It may be painful. But in our pain may be our profit and that of those to whom in future we shall preach.

"I can sense a reciprocal contact with the audience."

Ilse Joseph, the violinist,
in *Playing for Peace* (Temple
House Books, p. 74).

4
The Spirit, the Body, and the Word

When true preaching takes place, the main actor is — not the preacher, nor the congregation but — the Holy Spirit. That he uses men and women as his agents and fellow workers is true, and we shall have more to say about this shortly. But it is essential that we grasp the fact that, when an act of real preaching takes place, the most active part, the vital part of the enterprise, is taken by the third person of the blessed Trinity. Without him and his creative and recreative activity there can be words, there can be essays, there can be the "reading of a paper", but there can be no preaching. As the writer of the Fourth Gospel puts it, it is the function of the Holy Spirit to confute, to convict and to convince (John 16:8—11).

When a preacher grasps this, he discovers a cause for deep thankfulness, for he realizes that behind him are all the resources of God's greatness. Like Mrs Elizabeth Browning, he can

> "smile to think how God's greatness
> flowed round our incompleteness,
> round our restlessness
> his rest".

God is no niggardly giver — "so *measureless* is God's gift of the Spirit" (John 3:34); "that one Holy Spirit was *poured out* for all of us to drink" (1 Corinthians 12:13, NEB); "God's love has *flooded* our inmost heart through the Holy Spirit he has given us" (Romans 5:5).

When John speaks of the Holy Spirit as the Paraclete (in chapters 14—16 of his gospel), he uses a word which is notoriously difficult to translate. To transliterate the Greek and to confront the ordinary reader with the word "Paraclete" helps little. "Comforter" will not do in the twentieth century, for it has lost the powerful meaning which it had in the seventeenth, when the emphasis was on the second syllable (cp. *fortify*, *fortification*, etc.). "Counsellor" (Revised Standard Version), "helper" (J.B. Phillips, Good News Bible, and William Barclay), "Advocate" (New English Bible), and other translations all help. But they fail to convey the note of *stimulation* which is part of the meaning of the word (and of the verb from which it is derived) in the New Testament. Encouragement and enlivening of mind and perception — all this is inherent in this scintillating word. It is difficult to find an English translation to encompass its richness; perhaps "stimulator" or "awakener" would help. The French word *animateur* gets close to an element which, in the context of preaching, is highly significant. For it suggests that, as the preacher does his preparation or takes his stand in the pulpit, he is not alone. Beside him, within him, is the Stimulator-Spirit, the Lord, the Life-Giver, ready to enliven mind and speech, to alert to new truths, to re-vivify old concepts. The prime actor in the Sacrament of the Word is the Holy Spirit.

The Sacrament of the Eucharist provides us with a helpful comparison. In that central service of the Church certain elements, the elements of bread and wine, given to us by God, are presented by the people. "Through your goodness we have this bread to offer which earth has given and human hands have made." We pray that "by the power of your Holy Spirit these gifts of bread and wine may be to us his body and his blood", and that "as we eat and drink these holy gifts" God will "renew us by your Spirit, inspire us with your love, and unite us in the body of your Son."

So it is in preaching. The "elements" are words, ordinary words, the words that we constantly use in the commerce of everyday life. But in preaching, the life-giving Spirit takes these words and makes them the vehicles of his grace. He fashions words into the Word. Who can doubt that, when such preaching takes place, there is the Real Presence of Christ?

The preacher will, of course, always bear in mind that, when he thinks of words as the elements, the matter through which the Holy Spirit works in the activity of preaching, a unique place is to be given to the words of Scripture. This, as we saw in chapter 1, is symbolized by the giving of a Bible at his ordination to deacon, priest, and bishop. P.T. Forsyth, lecturing in 1907, put the point pithily: "The Bible, properly used, becomes, by the Holy Spirit's action, the sacramental book." (*Church and Sacrament*, p. 165). Professor C.E.B. Cranfield, writing some eighty years later, made much the same point even more forcefully: "To try to bypass the Bible in preaching is as perverse as attempting to celebrate the Holy Supper without bread or wine . . . it is, in fact, to show oneself ignorant of what preaching is all about" (*The Bible and Christian Life*, T.T. Clark, 1955, p. 12).

Here indeed is miracle and mystery. That is not surprising, for we are dealing with the incarnational principle, God's taking up of temporal things for the conveyance of eternal realities. We can only worship and adore.

It was a true insight on the part of those who drew up the Prayer Book of 1662 that the only place where a sermon was specifically ordered was in the service of Holy Communion. In so doing, they were insisting that the two sacramental acts should go together, both being dependent for their efficacy on the presence and activity of the Holy Spirit. Through both, God reaches the hearts of his people and "graces" them. Through both, the Church becomes the organ of insight so that its members can dare to say "it seemed good to the Holy Spirit and to us" (Acts 15:28) and to echo the words of Paul, "We have the mind of Christ" (1 Corinthians 2:16. Note the plural "we"; this is no claim for individualistic cocksureness, but a sober statement about the people of God enlightened and nourished by the Spirit).

Put at its simplest, sacraments are the means by which God brings home to us the reality of his redeeming love. In the sacraments of Baptism and Eucharist, the appeal is to the eye — these sacraments are God's *verba visibilia*. In the sacrament of the word, the appeal is to the ear — sermons are God's *verba audibilia*. Water, bread and wine are the stuff of baptism and eucharist. Words are the stuff of preaching. "The Word and the Sacraments belong together, one stimulating and enlivening the other, one nourishing and clothing the other in action" (Stephen

77

Bayne: *Enter with Joy*, Seabury Press, 1961, p. 91).

Luke would seem to have been saying something very like this in his story of the walk to and meal at Emmaus (chapter 24). Here were two disconsolate disciples (?man and wife) on the road. At the end of the walk, they asked Jesus into their home for a meal. He accepted. The guest became the host. He took the bread and said the blessing, broke it and offered it to them (v.30). They recalled how, on their walk with the Stranger, he had explained the Scriptures to them in such a way that their hearts burned within them. The supper became a sacrament. In the meal and on the road, broken bread and opened Bible were made vehicles of revelation and new life by the presence and activity of the Lord. Thus revivified, "without a moment's delay they set out . . . found that the Eleven and the rest of the company had assembled . . . and gave their account" (vv.33—35). Witness to the risen Lord was the natural sequence to participation in the sacrament of the Word and the sacrament of the table. The body, thus strengthened, became the agent of mission.

It is a matter of interest and a cause for thanksgiving that the Roman Catholic Church at the Second Vatican Council, in its *Constitution on the Sacred Liturgy*, apparently re-grasped this ancient emphasis. It was explicit about the importance of the proclamation of the word of God. It spoke of "the two parts which in a sense go to make up the Mass, viz. the liturgy of the word and the eucharistic liturgy", and it went on to say that these two parts are "so closely connected with each other that they form but one single act of worship" (56). Indeed, the homily "is to be highly esteemed as part of the liturgy itself. In fact at those Masses which are celebrated on Sundays and holy days of obligation, with the people assisting, it should not be omitted except for a serious reason" (52).

❖

This stress on the Holy Spirit as the main actor in preaching does not for one moment diminish the importance of the human factor. Indeed, it enhances it. It does so in respect both of the preacher and in respect of the congregation. Both have their part to play. Let us consider them in that order.

The preacher. Just before entering the pulpit, the preacher kneels to pray. What is he doing? He is offering, and asking. He is *offering* to God the work that he has done on his sermon during the week, the fruit of his toil, the labour of mind and heart. He is conscious that in itself it is a poor thing, indeed, apart from God's action, a useless thing. But he offers it. And he is *asking* that the Holy Spirit will do his creative work, will take, bless, and break the word, will confute, convict and convince, will illuminate mind, touch conscience, scatter darkness, bring light. "Lord, take it such as it is, and make it what you would have it to be and to do."

In thus offering and asking, he is conscious of the fact that he is a fellow worker with God. God the Spirit and he the preacher are going into action together. He has no authority of his own; he is at the receiving end of an authority given him by God. He is in a great succession and is "engaged", as P.T. Forsyth put it, "on the Gospel prolonging and declaring itself". For "every true sermon . . . is a sacramental time and act. It is God's Gospel act re-asserting itself in detail . . . It is a sacramental act, done together with the community in the name and power of Christ's redeeming act and our common faith". (*Positive Preaching and the Modern Mind*, p. 83).

The congregation. We have said that the *congregation*, and not only the preacher, has a part to play in preaching. This needs to be defined with some care. It is for lack of understanding at this point that many of our people have a low estimate of preaching, if indeed they have thought about it in any depth at all.

We have made the point that preaching is an activity of the Holy Spirit. It is obviously an activity of the preacher. But it is also an activity of the Church as the Body of Christ and of the congregation gathered in such and such a place Sunday by Sunday. The members of the church are themselves "workers together with God" when preaching takes place, working together with the Holy Spirit and with the man or woman in the pulpit. Three actors are engaged – Holy Spirit, preacher, and person in pew. Preaching is not simply the man up there doing his act. In preaching, the *Church* goes into action.

How? Most obviously, the people in the pew come *prayerfully*. A well-taught congregation knows that much of the quality of the worship (sermon included) depends on the prayerfulness of those who come to the service. Much depends on the quiet waiting on God before the service begins. Then, at the point of the sermon, there will be prayerful co-operation between the people in the pew and the person in the pulpit. "May his words and our thinking be acceptable in your sight, O Lord, our strength and our redeemer."

Then there will be the co-operation of *minds*. Perhaps God will reveal some truth never seen before, or only dimly glimpsed. The Christian faith is vast; is there some new aspect of it to be seen today, or some old truth to be more firmly grasped? "Come, Holy Ghost our *minds* inspire, And lighten with celestial fire" — that is a translation of the old Latin hymn more accurate than the one with which we are familiar.

The preacher may not be a brilliant intellectual. Many in the congregation may well be better educated than he. But often, by God's inspiration, he will "spark off" a train of thought, or open up a new vista of truth, which a listener with mind erect to God will be able to follow up to his own profit and the good of his fellows.

Then there will be the readiness of *will* to put into action any demand which the preaching will suggest. Prayer and mental activity will lead to obedience. Life will reflect the truth that has been learned.

Along lines such as these, co-operation will take place between pulpit and pew, and we shall see the truth of Kierkegaard's dictum that "in preaching

> God is the audience;
> *The listeners are the actors*;
> The preacher is the prompter."

Kierkegaard's idea of God as audience is not, I think, a contradiction of our insistence that God is the great actor in preaching. It is, rather, a reminder that the preacher must bear in mind the fact that there is an unseen Listener as he speaks; he can, therefore, be no "respecter of persons", since the main auditor is always God himself! In saying that the listeners are the actors, he makes the point on which we are insisting and which we must now develop, that preaching is the function of the *Church*, and the preacher is a "prompter" enabling it to fulfil its function.

In recent decades, in a great many churches in both the Anglican and Roman Catholic traditions, the focal point of the Eucharist, the Holy Table, has been removed from the far east end of the church building and brought down to a more central position. The reason for this is not merely to ensure better audibility or visibility, though these matters are important: the central acts of taking, blessing, breaking, and giving should be seen and watched by the congregation. The reason for this re-arrangement of furniture is to manifest the point that the Eucharist is the act not only of the celebrant "away up there", but of the whole Body of Christ gathered in that place. "*Do* this in remembrance of me" is addressed to all present at the Family meal. Dom Gregory Dix, in his *The Shape of the Liturgy* (pp. 29–30), writing about early eucharistic worship, said: "*The whole Church* prayed in the Person of Christ; the *whole Church* was charged with the office of 'proclaiming' the revelation of Christ; the *whole Church* offered the eucharist as the 're-calling' before God and man of the offering of Christ . . . Christ and his Church are one, with one mission, one life, one prayer, one Gospel, one offering, one being, one Father." Sunday by Sunday the laity come to the Eucharist, not as spectators but as performers of the liturgy.

If this is true of the Eucharist, it is equally true of that other sacrament, the sacrament of the word. The act of preaching is not something done to us by the man up there in the pulpit, any more than the Holy Communion is an act done by the man who stands at the altar. The members of the congregation share in the act of preaching just as they share in the central act of the Eucharist. Both acts are acts of the Body corporate, every member in his own office having his own function to perform. In the early Church it would seem that the task of the president was both to preach the word and to break the bread. Only when the

Church grasps this anew shall we see preaching as the holy thing which in truth it is.

We have made much in this chapter of the fact that the true preacher is not a solitary performer; that when preaching takes place, the Holy Spirit and the preacher are co-workers; that preacher and people also are workers together with God the Spirit and with one another. In fact, there is a trinity of activity — God and preacher and congregation.

In considering the part played by the congregation when preaching takes place, I shall call to our aid some interesting parallels from the world of music. There are parallels between the activity of preacher and congregation and the activity of, say, a pianist and his audience, which are suggestive and helpful. Nor should this be a matter for surprise. There are things in the realm of the spirit which can be done by music which cannot be done by words. Great music *says* things which words cannot convey. (This is true also in the realm of dance — "Do you think I would have danced it if I could have said it?", Pavlova is reported to have replied to an enquirer who wanted to know the meaning of her act.) Have not most of us experienced moments when we have been lifted out of depression and out of almost-despair by the performance of some great musical work? "If *that* be so," we say, "all must be well at the heart of the universe." We have returned to our work with a livelier hope and a deeper conviction that Julian of Norwich was right — "All shall be well and all shall be well, and all manner of thing shall be well"; we have a firmer faith than before that God's "hidden purpose . . . that the universe . . . be brought into a unity in Christ" will, in fact, "be put into effect" (Ephesians 1:9–10). The conviction of the Psalmists that music is an integral part of religious worship points to the fact that the Creator works through music as well as through words (see, among many examples, Psalms 57:8; 149:1–3; 150:3–6). We should, therefore, not be surprised to find that the experience of great musicians will aid preachers in their task of conveying God's truth to men. Let us look at specific examples.

On 2 March 1986, on B.B.C. television, I listened to Vladimir Ashkenazy playing the soloist's part as André Previn conducted the Royal Philharmonic Orchestra in a performance of Beethoven's Fourth Piano Concerto. I watched Ashkenazy almost with awe. As I did so, I saw a man who — is this putting it too strongly? — was in communion with Beethoven. No doubt for decades he had studied and practised the scores of his works. But there was more to the performance than a mere production of the notes which Beethoven had put down on paper. It seemed that the spirit of the master had entered into and had got hold of the disciple. Ashkenazy was wholly Beethoven's man; in a manner of speaking, he had become one with him. There was something of Paul's "it is no longer I that live: Christ lives in me" (Galatians 2:20).

The result of this unity of spirit, this deep understanding, was to be seen in the man at the piano being wonderfully at rest. The concerto was long and complicated, a mighty mixture of the gentle and the powerful. The opportunities for disaster on the part of the pianist were manifold — suppose he forgot this phrase or that?; suppose he came in a fraction too early or too late? But here was a man quietly confident: there was a unity between performer and composer so close that a breakdown seemed well nigh inconceivable. This was more than a feat of memory. It was a unity of mind and spirit, a unity of desire and action.

So much, then, for the relationship of master Beethoven and performer-disciple Ashkenazy (of the Holy Spirit and the preacher). What about the relationship of the performer and the audience (of the preacher and the congregation)? Let us turn for our example to another pianist, Alfred Brendel.

On 24 July 1982, again on television, I watched Bernard Levin interviewing the great Brendel. He asked him about the interaction of pianist and audience. Brendel replied: "It is like an electric stream that goes into the audience and comes back again, *and greatly enhances what the pianist does.*" He was speaking of a relationship, hard to define in words but best expressed in terms of electricity, which was real and vital. Clearly, his audience was more than a body of people at whom, so to speak, he threw his music. Rather, in their receptivity they were also co-operating with him, and the result was not only their enrichment but the enhancement of his performance.

Few men and women who have been long at the task of

preaching can fail to miss the point of Brendel's reply to Levin. We have all known those dreadful occasions when we have had *no* come-back from the congregation — the electric stream goes out but does not come back, and there is no enhancement of what the preacher does! The reasons for this deadness may be many. We ourselves may not have been in touch with the Master; or our preparation may have been deficient; or our relationship with others may have been wrong; all these things block the flow of the current and must be taken into consideration. But sometimes — I believe often — the reason for the deadness is that our people have never been taught that preaching is a function of the Church and not simply of "the man up there"; that three are concerned, the Spirit, the preacher, and the man in the pew. The preacher must teach, and go on teaching, about what preaching really is. Unless he does, his listeners will be sufferers (some less patient than others!) rather than collaborators. "The preacher who genuinely believes preaching is the activity of the whole congregation will not only develop the skills for a style of preaching which makes that possible but will also be patient while the listeners *overcome years of quiet submission* to some-one else's conclusions" (F.B. Craddock: *Preaching*, Abingdon Press, Nashville, 1985, p. 26; italics mine).

There is a very practical aspect to this matter of the rela-tionship of the preacher to the people and their responding relationship to him. "While we preach we will receive countless signals in body language and in other ways of how the faithful are responding to what we are saying. That means that we should never be so bound to a manuscript that we lose our freedom to respond to the messages we are receiving from the faces turned toward us" (O.C. Edwards, Jr.: *Elements of Homiletic*, Pueblo Publishing Company, New York, 1982, p. 97). The preacher is, in a real sense, a conductor, helping his people in the activity of preaching as they help him. We have already noticed Kierke-gaard's description of the preacher as "the prompter" (which is close to "conductor"). Here again the musicians help us.

Recently, I watched André Previn conducting. He had the score open before him. Very occasionally he glanced at it. With a mere flick of the hand he turned the pages. That was all. So he was free to engage with the members of the orchestra, free to co-operate with the soloist in an easy liaison. He was in such rapport with the master whose work he was conducting, and he knew his score so well, that there was no need to be bound to the pages before him. He was free to receive the signals from the orchestra and to draw out from them all the riches that they had to give. To watch this was an essay in close and fruitful co-operation.

In Levin's interview with Brendel, Brendel told Levin that, when performing the work of a great composer, he "did not want *to be in the way of the composer*". And Levin, commenting about a series of recitals of Beethoven's sonatas which the pianist gave in 1977, wrote: "All the way through we have been transfixed not by the performer's art but by the composer's — the last test, and the most searching of all. Brendel vanishes behind the music . . . " It was obviously clear to those who heard the pianist at work that Beethoven had made a profound impression on him, done something to him at the deepest level of his personality, and that it was his passionate desire to pass on that something to his audience. Brendel magnified Beethoven. Brendel, getting out of the way of Beethoven, manifested the greatness of Beethoven.

We noted a little earlier in this chapter that Ashkenazy, in playing a long and complicated work, seemed "wonderfully at rest . . . quietly confident". That seems to be one of the marks of those who are masters of their art, and it is deeply significant. But at the end of his performance, there was sweat on his forehead! It was clear that "power had gone out of him", as it went out of Jesus in his healing activity (Mark 5:30). A performance is a costly act to a musician, and it is not to be wondered at if the preacher's signature in the vestry book is sometimes shaky! Paul, who makes much of the "peace of God which passes all understanding" and which garrisons heart and mind (Philippians 4:7), also writes of Christian discipleship in terms of athletic striving (the word for "athlete" in 1 Corinthians 9:25 is, if transliterated, the *agonizer*) and of "striving with all the energy which [Christ] mightily inspires within me" (Colossians 1:29 — it is the same word as in 1 Corinthians 9:25). There were long hours, long years, of unremitting discipline and practice behind Ashkenazy's "artless" performance; and even on the night itself the performance *cost*. There was an element of passion in it, and passion means suffering. This is true in the realm of music; it is equally true in the realm of preaching. I noted in a recent speech by the historian Dame Veronica Wedgwood her insistence on "passion without which no major work can be written". We might go further and say: "passion without which no great piece of music can be performed", and "passion without which no great sermon can be preached".

There is a world of difference between histrionics and passion. The former has about it a note of the artificial, of the insincere; the latter, a note of reality, of sincerity, of depth. At a young musicians" competition recently, the judge, commenting on the performance of a girl aged fourteen, said: "The performance was immensely competent but *lacking in heart*. That will come later." We know what he meant. In art, in music, in preaching, competence is necessary and to be toiled for. But "heart", as the judge called it, comes only from communion with God and from entering into the joys and sorrows of our fellow human beings. Competence must be married to compassion.

We have been insisting that in preaching there is an inter-relationship between the person in the pulpit and the people in the pew — a reciprocal contact which has immense creative and re-creative possibilities. It is my own belief that, if these possibilities are to be realized and maximized, there will have to be opportunities for closer interchange after the sermon is over. It may well be that many in the congregation will not feel the need for this nor will they want it. But the intelligent listener, the seeker, the perplexed may want to make some come-back, to make some verbal contribution of his own, to ask for some clarification, to make some criticism, to want a re-play of the sermon for purposes of better digestion. This, surely, is the place for the informal study group to be held after the service or, more probably, during the course of the week. Of this we shall have more to say in the next chapter.

Lord, take this sermon, such as it is,
and make it what you would have it to be
and to do.

May my words and our thinking
be acceptable in your sight,
O Lord, our strength and our redeemer.

May I speak
and may we hear
the word of God.

"Then those who feared the Lord talked together, and the Lord paid heed and listened"

Malachi 3:16

5

Preaching and Dialogue

"Dialogue" in the context of this book means an opportunity for conversation between the preacher and members of the congregation who have heard his sermon; discussion in some depth; an open exchange of views; the opportunity for the listeners to question the preacher; and a chance for them to make positive contributions *both* to what has been said in the pulpit on a specific occasion *and* to the whole preaching ministry of the church in that particular place. This takes further the theme which we have already elaborated, that one of the most important parts in the activity of preaching is the part taken by the men and women in the pew.

"Dialogue" is a good word which has been much abused. It has become so popular in some church circles that it has sometimes worn thin and come to mean little more than wordy exchange by people who know little about the particular subject; it is argument based on little substance. So a noble word can come to signify a wasteland, beginning in desert and ending in vacuity.

But "dialogue" is ennobled by its use in the New Testament, particularly in the Acts of the Apostles and in relation to Paul's work (see p. 67 above). A study of the occurrence of the verb *dialegomai* gives some interesting results (it occurs in 17:2 and 17; 18:4 and 19; 19:8 and 9; 20:7 and 9; 24:25). It shows us the apostle engaging in argument and discussion, in disputing and reasoning, *both* in the synagogues where he would have expounded his message based on Hebrew Scriptures and the recent "Christ-event", *and* in non-Jewish circles, at Athens, at Tyrannus's "school", and with the Roman governor Felix (on "morals, self-control and the coming judgement"). In spite of Paul's general policy of moving on, after a brief stay, from one centre to another on his evangelistic work, he was content to remain at Ephesus for more than two years to give full rein to the opportunities presented by dialogue. We can hear the thrust and parry of debate, the interchange of minds, the passion of persuasion. Paul was not content with monologue: there must be opportunity for lively come-back. (Only Eutychus is recorded as ever having succeeded in going to sleep while Paul was in full flood! — 20:9.) Time and patience must be allowed for dialogue — no pressures of other work must cut it short. The people must *really* be listened to, their beliefs and feelings *really* be appreciated.

Our troubles begin when we seek to play off "dialogue" against "declaration", interchange of mind and speech against proclamation. This has happened all too often, and we need to take a look at the matter.

There was a time not long ago — indeed, the argument is still heard in certain quarters — when it was said, if not in so many words, in effect: "It is not possible profitably to engage in proclamation. At this period of the Church's history, the preacher can do little more than ask questions and hope that they are the right ones. Preaching, in the sense of declaring, proclaiming, announcing good news, has largely had its day. Today is the day of dialogue in which the participants ask one another questions, share experiences, doubts and feelings, and hope that truth will emerge. The pulpit must give place to the discussion group, the church to the coffee-room, and the idea of a man or woman authorized by the Body of Christ to 'preach the word' should give way to that of one seeker for truth joining others in the search — that and little more."

This will not do — and for several reasons. *First*, we must mention the abysmal ignorance of even the basics of the Christian faith which is the lot of the vast majority of people in the West towards the end of the twentieth century. Listen to a general knowledge quiz on any radio programme, and you find the most elementary questions on the Christian faith or on the Bible left unanswered. Ask any school-teacher how much their pupils know of these things, and the answers point to a lack of knowledge which is nothing less than astounding. It is not possible to hold intelligent dialogue with such people unless and until some teaching has been done; to do so would be like trying to make bricks without straw. Even within the congregations of church people the level of ignorance is often high (a fact which itself raises questions about the nature of the pulpit ministry which they have "*sat under*" (sic!), often for long years). Intelligent dialogue must have some solid base of knowledge from which it can emerge; otherwise it ceases to be intelligent, and results in hot air.

Secondly, the services of ordination are largely evacuated of their meaning if "declaration" is out and only "dialogue" is in. "Take thou Authority to preach the Word of God . . . " "Receive this book; here are words of eternal life. Take them for your guide, and declare them to the world . . . " "Receive this Bible as a sign of the authority given you to preach the Word of God and to administer his holy Sacraments." We have examined these things in an earlier chapter (pp. 21ff). We need do no more than mention them again here.

Thirdly, to substitute dialogue for proclamation is to fly in the face of the evidence of the New Testament. No one can honestly read the Acts of the Apostles and the letters of Paul (to mention only two of the main strata of these writings) without gaining an overwhelming impression that the members of the young Church went on their way with the strongest possible sense of mission, with a message to proclaim, with a faith to expound, with an experience to share. That message found its focus in "Jesus and the resurrection", the tremendous events of the incarnate, crucified and risen Lord through whom (to quote another stratum) members of the Church had been given "new birth into a living hope by the resurrection of Jesus Christ from the dead" (1 Peter 1:3). Those events had changed the course of world history; a new age had dawned. Hope had taken the place of despair; darkness had given way to light. Put the apostles in prison and caution them to keep silent, and they can only reply: "We cannot possibly give up speaking of things we have seen and heard" (Acts 4:20). The thrill of discovery comes through in the opening words of John's first letter: "It was there from the beginning; we have heard it; we have seen it with our own eyes;

we looked upon it, and felt it with our own hands; and it is of this we tell. Our theme is the word of life." This was a treasure beyond all price, and it was given to be shared. Keep it to themselves and they would lose it. Share it, and they would receive it back immensely enriched. They were trustees of a message which must be proclaimed from the housetops. For the Church to fail in this task would be to rob it of its claim to be the Church at all.

Has something happened in the years that have intervened between the salad days of the Church's history and our own, that now we can only ask questions, engage in dialogue, tentatively put out suggestions for discussion? Or is the very idea a subtle way of pulling the carpet from under the preacher's feet and draining the power from his message?

To hint that there is a choice to be made, in this sophisticated age, between the "old" method of proclamation and the "new" method of dialogue is to face the preacher with a false antithesis which is to be scorned. Let him have none of it! Let him opt for both!

The idea of proclamation with authority behind it does not mean that the preacher will face his congregation as a kind of Mr Know-all who has pat answers wrapped up in readiness for those who want to ask him questions. He himself will enter the pulpit as a man with many questions to which he has no answer or only the hint of an answer. Nor will he be ashamed to acknowledge this to those who listen to him. Life is full of perplexity and it is no good hiding the fact or trying to run away from it. Probably his congregation would despise him if they found him doing this. But while this will be made plain from his whole stance in the pulpit, the main thrust of that pulpit ministry will be positive, affirmative. "What we have seen and heard we declare to you, so that you and we together may share in a common life, that life which we share with the Father and his Son Jesus Christ" (1 John 1:3).

This will be the foundation of a preaching-and-teaching ministry which, over the years, will build up the Church, and enable its members to face, unafraid, the questions of a sceptical and (often) wistful world.

Against that background, is it possible to spell out the place for dialogue in relation to preaching in the context of a parish? Let us try.

I have in mind a parish where the preaching ministry is undertaken with the seriousness which it deserves. It is seen as an important element of each Sunday's worship of heart and mind on the part of the preacher and of the congregation. The preacher knows that he has much to give. The members of the congregation know that they, too, have much to contribute. But, the sermon being over, the act of worship concluded, what then? It is here, I believe, that dialogue comes into its own honourable and valuable place — dialogue which will enrich both the preacher and the members of the congregation.

The people of God, the laity, have much to give. Each member of the Body of Christ has a contribution to make. Each has some experience of God's grace coming to them in Christ, the gifts of the Spirit differing from each other in a wide variety. The laity have a knowledge of the world, of men and affairs, which the clergy sometimes lack. They know the questions which their friends in business or in the professions or in the shops are actually asking. (It was William Temple who used to say that some clergy are experts at answering questions that people never ask. And there was the cartoon in an old issue of *Punch* which depicted an ancient clergyman leaning over the edge of the pulpit and saying to a handful of rustics in the pews: "Ah! I think I hear you say, 'Anti-Sabellianism?' ".) The laity will not only save us from making fools of ourselves in matters which we are not trained to understand; they will also suggest to us subjects which we need to deal with in the round of our preaching work.

Someone who lives close to the soil will enrich me if he will share with me some of Nature's secrets. A doctor's insight into human griefs and weaknesses; a teacher's knowledge of the young and their joys and sorrows; a policeman's intimacy with the seamier side of life; a psychiatrist's knowledge of what makes us tick; a mother's familiarity with home and family life; a woman's percipience and sureness of touch; a craftsman's patience in the handling of his material; a musician's experience of discipline and inspiration; the wisdom of old age; the impatience of youth — these are all gifts of the Spirit given for our enrichment as individuals and for the building up of Christ's Body. Suppose that all or some of these people will share these gifts with me, the preacher, in the give-and-take of dialogue, shall I not be greatly enriched? And will not my preaching take on a fuller flavour, while at the same time it is more securely earthed? In listening humbly and attentively to another person, I shall be able to hear the voice of God. The sermon, thus enriched, will be a worthier offering next Sunday to the God whom preacher and listeners seek to worship.

Again, the co-operation of the people with the preacher will save the latter from certain pitfalls into which he can all too easily fall. I have mentioned the danger of answering questions which rarely occur to the people in the pew. Another danger is the use of language to which they are unaccustomed and which they do not understand. Let it be granted that, if we are en route to Zion, we have to learn the language of Zion. Just as a scientist has a language which he must use if he is to talk about his particular branch of learning, so has the theologian and the preacher; and he will have to teach the elements of that language to his people. But I need to listen to the member of my congregation who will be good enough to say to me, in the course of our dialogue: "You used a phrase I did not understand, or a word I had never heard before." (Who was the preacher who began his address: "I want to speak to you about the Paraclete"; whereupon a member of the congregation whispered to his neighbour, "Why does he want to preach about that bird?") Is is too much to ask that, if I develop, as so easily I can, some maddening habit of voice or hands, someone will be kind and honest enough to tell me?

This sharing of experience and this attitude of frankness on the part of the laity with the clergy presupposes a humility on the part of the latter which is itself a gift of the Spirit. Some of us are not open to take this without an element of resentment — "after all", we say, at least to ourselves, "we are the experts". The result will be our own impoverishment. But if we are humble enough to see that such give-and-take is part of that fellowship which is itself a mark of the Spirit's presence in our community, each phrase of the prayer "The grace of our Lord Jesus Christ, and the love of God, and the fellowship of the Holy Spirit" will be filled with a new content. Our receptivity and openness will yield a high dividend.

Interchange of this kind will be retrospective and prospective. It will be *retrospective*; for those who meet to pursue dialogue will look back to the sermon of the previous Sunday, or to the sermons of the preceding month if meetings take place at intervals of some weeks. Here it will be the course of wisdom to play over all or part of the sermon which is being discussed on the tape which was made when the sermon was preached. The making of such tapes is a very simple operation and can well be undertaken by a member of the congregation as the contribution of his particular talent to the whole operation of preaching. These aids to efficiency and edification are now at our disposal; it is a great pity not to use them. It will be *prospective*; for preacher and congregation will be looking forward to the sermons of the coming weeks and months. As the discussion develops, points will emerge where help is clearly needed. Subjects will suggest themselves. Requests will be made. Misunderstandings of a previous sermon will need a sermon, or even a series of sermons, for correction and enlightenment. The preacher himself will find, as he listens to the tape of last Sunday's sermon, that there were points there on which he was able only to touch but which call for elaboration and explication. It is likely that the notebook in which the preacher makes jottings for future pulpit work will find itself used more frequently and more profitably because of the repeat of the sermon on the tape and because of the comments of those who engage in dialogue about it.

A friend of mine, who is as humble as he is learned, tells me that from time to time he used to enlist the help of his undergraduate friends in the preparation of the sermons which he was to preach in the College chapel. Having prepared the first draft on his own, he would share it with them, encouraging them to criticize it and to make suggestions as to its improvement and enrichment. Might a similar experiment be worth trying out in some parishes where the preacher has a small group of friends whose spiritual insight he has learnt to value? Joint preparation and collective criticism, in such cases, could be fruitful.

Dialogue of this kind will, no doubt, help to answer many questions. That will be good. But it will also raise many others, and that could be even better. It will create appetite of mind and spirit. The participants in the dialogue will begin to understand what the Psalmist said when he cried out, "O God, thou art my God, I seek thee early with a heart that thirsts for thee and a body wasted with longing for thee, like a dry and thirsty land that has no water" (63:1). Addressing himself to the people in the pew, the Revd Richard A. Bower, of Trinity Church, Princeton, New Jersey, recently wrote: "Like most matters of faith, preaching is meant to deepen questions more than produce answers. No preacher can work it all out for you. Responsibility and decision rest in your lap (or heart). So when we as preachers are doing our job, we are holding up the light of God's Word (with a minimum of our own light) in ways that leave you the work to do, the response to make, the new questions to bring, the new hope to act upon." That certainly was the way that Jesus preached and taught, often refusing to answer a direct question with a direct answer but, instead, telling a story and leaving the hearer to make a response of mind or will — the ball had been put right into his or her court.

Precisely how or when this element of dialogue will happen can only be defined within the particular setting of the place where the preaching is done. In some cases, it will take place on the Sunday morning on which the sermon has been delivered. The pattern might be a Eucharist with sermon fairly early, followed by coffee, and then, for those who wish to remain, a period of discussion. This would have the advantage that the sermon would be fresh in the minds of the hearers; there would be no need to play it over on the tape. This sermon plus discussion would fit into the programme of religious education which occupies a large part of the Sunday morning especially in the churches of North America, and could prove very profitable.

But for many that pattern would prove impossible. There are people who must hurry home after the morning service — children or old people must be cared for, the Sunday meal must be cooked. For such, some provision must be made in the week. The members will meet in a parish hall or in the lounge or the kitchen of a house. This is by no means a second-best time. The interval from Sunday to, say, Wednesday has allowed time for the sermon to be thought over and digested. The playing of the tape will freshen the memory, and the members will be well on the way to a fruitful hour.

How often should such meetings take place? Here again, there will be a wide variety of answers to the question. Perhaps once a week will be right in certain places. But once a fortnight or once a month may well prove more helpful in others. To have two, three, or even four sermons to think about and to discuss may provide richer fare and lead to richer dialogue.

Whichever day is decided upon, and wherever the dialogue takes place, it would probably be well, at least at the start, to limit the sessions to the duration of something like an academic term. Suppose that the sessions took place in October and November. The participants could then have a rest, and resume, if they felt it right, for more meetings in, say, January and February. Such limitations would prevent staleness. All too many groups sicken and die simply because the series of meetings goes on too long.

A final word must be said about the spirit in which dialogue takes place. The purpose of the meetings is, first and last, the sharing of the gifts of the members of the group for the building up of the Body of Christ. Preacher and members of the congregation meet to ensure that that part of the weekly worship which is preaching shall steadily become a worthier offering to Almighty God.

These are wholly positive ends — *sharing*, *building the Body*, *worthier offering*. The members do not meet to pull last Sunday's sermon to pieces (though they may be critical). Nor do they meet to flatter the preacher (though they will not be slow to encourage). Preacher and members of the congregation meet to work together to answer such questions as these: "What *is* preaching?" (This is a basic question which might well be tackled before dialogue takes place on any particular sermon. We shall have more to say about this in the next chapter.) "What is the part of the laity in preaching?" "What is the purpose of a sermon?" These basic questions having been wrestled with, the group can then go on to look at last Sunday's sermon (or the previous two, three or four sermons). "How did that sermon stand up to what the group had discovered in tackling the earlier questions? What were its strong points or its weak points from the angle of the preacher and from the input of the congregation? Was there a strong element of teaching? What place was given to Scripture? Was the language such as could be understood by people who were not theologically literate?" We could go on suggesting questions, but it would be better for the group itself to work out the main questions which they would wish to address to the sermon to which they have listened.

The success of such dialogue can readily be measured. If, over a period, it produces a group of men and women who have caught a vision of what preaching is in the mind of God; if that group becomes a *praying* group devoted to the sharing of their gifts, to the building up of the Body, to the making of a worthier offering to God; and if the preacher finds in that group a source of strength as he does his part in study and pulpit, then success will have been achieved. If these results have not been achieved, or are not in process of being achieved, the raison d'être of the group should be re-considered. Is is truly fulfilling its purpose?

Take our minds, and think through them.
Take our lips, and speak through them.
Take our hearts, and set them on fire with love for thee.
What we know not, teach us.
What we have not, give us.
What we are not, make us.
For Jesus Christ's sake.

"I hate definitions."

Benjamin Disraeli

6
Towards a Definition of Preaching

It is a wholesome exercise for each of us who engages in preaching to sit down with a blank sheet of paper before us and to write on that paper our own definition of preaching. What *is* this thing on which we engage, some of us regularly, some of us occasionally? Can we state it in a sentence or two, in non-technical language? If we cannot, our inability to do so may point to one reason for the ineffectiveness of what we do in the pulpit — aim at nothing and you will hit it!

The task will not be easy. As we work at the defining in the light of the actual performing, it may well be that our definition will be different in twelve months" time from what it is now. That will be a healthy sign — we are growing in theory and in practice. Further, your definition may be different from mine, for you approach preaching from your point of view and I from mine. That, again, is good, for we learn from one another. That is why we keep reading books about preaching, and keep reading the sermons of others. We share God's gifts in this great sphere of thinking and speaking.

The purpose of this chapter is not to provide the preacher with a ready-made definition of preaching. Rather, its aim is to look at a few definitions and to draw out from them certain elements without the inclusion of which any attempt at definition on our part would be obviously defective. By no means all the essential elements will be included in any one of these definitions — it will be for us to supply some more, as our thinking moves us. Let the heading of this chapter be noted — "*towards* a definition . . . ." It is for the reader to draw up his own answer, on the understanding that, later on, he will almost certainly find himself in need of revising it.

Phillips Brooks' definition of preaching as "the bringing of truth through personality" is, of course, patently inadequate, and he, no doubt, would have been the first to grant this. It is a description of one aspect of preaching rather than a definition of it, and Phillips Brooks' famous Lyman Beecher Lectures delivered in 1877 make that clear.

But that description is a good point at which to begin our search for a definition. It is good because it fastens on the *personality* of the preacher as being an essential element in preaching. P.T. Forsyth, whom we have quoted before in a different context, spoke of Christian preaching as "the sacrament of a consecrated personality". It may be true — indeed, I believe it is — that, in the words of Article XXVI, "the Unworthiness of the Ministers . . . hinders not the effect of the Sacrament"; the reference here is, of course, to the sacraments of Baptism and the Lord's Supper. Such is the power of the grace of God that in the sacrament of the Word, too, God's truth comes through sinful men and women and effectively results in blessing to those who hear. If that were not so, none of us would dare to preach. But, in the sacrament of the Word, there is so close a connection between the truth preached and him who preaches it, that the element of "consecrated personality" must be taken with the utmost seriousness. To put it positively, the holiness of the preacher affects the quality of the preaching in a terribly intimate way. This is not to deny the fact that the grace of God is such that it can take the utterance even of a wicked person and, by a miracle, use it to further God's mighty purpose. But such a miracle does not contradict the general principle that in preaching there is a kind of incarnation of the word which requires a holy person for its effectiveness. If that is a bit terrifying, as the writer found it to be as he wrote the words on the paper before him, it serves simply to cast the preacher wholly on the forgiving grace of the Lord who cleanses, authorizes, and sends his preachers.

"Truth *through personality*". My personality is one of God's most gracious gifts to me. It is unique. Just as there are no two people with the same finger-prints, so there are no two people with the same personalities. The distinctiveness is God's *charisma*, and he wills to use it distinctively in his service and not least in the ministry of the word. That is why it is wrong for anyone to seek to copy another preacher. Most of us have known men who have so modelled themselves on another that we can hear the other person and recognize him in their utterances. To copy and to mimic in this way is to do something destructive to one's own God-given uniqueness.

As God's truth comes to me and passes through me to others, something happens to me as well as to it. To be a channel (to use a word much loved in a certain type of piety) is not to be a funnel. A funnel is defined as "a hollow utensil with a wide mouth tapering to a small hole"! "Funnel" won't do. "Channel" is little better. "Agent" is nearer the mark; for through an agent something happens and is achieved, and this not in spite of him but through him. The musician — absorbing, performing, interpreting, giving, enjoying, sweating — is something more than a funnel or even a channel.

A personality, accepted at the hands of God just as it is with all its deficiencies received at birth or picked up on the journey, and then handed back to God for re-fashioning, that is a thing to be rejoiced in. It is not to be minimized or effaced, but to be purified and heightened and used in "the sacrament of a consecrated personality".

It is clear that, in our attempt to reach a definition of preaching, we are beginning with the person of the preacher. That is no bad thing. James Black described preaching as "the natural overflow of our religion". If there is no depth of *religion* in the preacher, if he is not a dedicated man, he can theorize but he can scarcely preach. (We are back at the theme of "giving a paper" which we touched on at the beginning of this book.) George Herbert captured the point in these verses:

> Lord, how can man preach thy eternal word?
>   He is a brittle little glass:
> Yet in thy temple thou dost him afford
>   This glorious and transcendent place
> To be a window, through thy grace.
>
> But where thou dost anneal in glass thy storie,
>   Making thy life to shine within

The holy preachers; then the light and glorie
　More rev"rend grows, and more doth win;
Which else shows waterish, bleak and thin.

So much for the second part of Phillips Brooks' definition. What about the first part, "*the bringing of truth*"? What is "truth" in this context? We might well begin our answer to this question by spelling "truth" with a capital T. This would have the effect of ensuring the centrality of Christ in preaching, Christ himself who is "the Way, the *Truth* and the Life". We proceed from Phillips Brooks' definition, which in itself begs so many questions, to another much more searching definition, that of Bernard L. Manning. To him, preaching was "a manifestation of the Incarnate Word, from the Written Word, by the spoken word" (*A Layman in the Ministry*, p. 138). This does not mean that every sermon must deal with Christology! A fully-rounded preaching ministry will deal with the Fatherhood of God, the person and work of the Holy Spirit, the nature of the Body of Christ and of the sacraments . . . ; it will seek to spell out the ethical outcome of these beliefs and their relevance to this life and the next. A huge vista of truth is envisaged as awaiting exploration and explication. But in stating that preaching is "a manifestation of the Incarnate Word", a showing forth of Christ, Manning is saying that a truly Christian programme of preaching will "home in" on the Word made flesh as surely as the needle of a compass points to the magnetic north. Again and again such a preacher will find himself returning to the Person of Christ, incarnate, crucified, risen, glorified, present among us, coming to us. He will understand how John Wesley could write in his journal for 17 July 1739: "I rode to Bradford five miles from Bath. Some persons had pitched on a convenient place, on the top of the hill under which the town lies . . . There I offered Christ to about a thousand people, for wisdom, righteousness, sanctification and redemption." That was simply an illustration of Wesley at his life-work, which he himself described as being that of "a man sent from God to persuade men to put Jesus Christ at the centre of their relationships".

Here we are getting very close to the heart of the matter. There is a passage in the Fourth Gospel which speaks of the Holy Spirit as "the Spirit of truth" who "will guide you into all the truth . . . He will glorify me . . . " (16:13—14). The Spirit's main concern, if we may put it this way, is to take of the things which have to do with Jesus and make them realities to us. It is the preacher's supreme responsibility to see to it that the Spirit has the material to work on. When this is so, when Christ is the central theme of the preaching, then there is opportunity for preaching to be seen for what in truth it is — *God at work*, God fashioning words into the Word. If Jesus Christ is himself the Gospel, then preaching must be a manifestation of that Gospel. Without him, the whole Christian scheme of things falls to pieces. With him at the centre, all things cohere. It is in this sense that P.T. Forsyth can speak of preaching as "the Gospel prolonging and declaring itself".

"*Manifestation*" — Manning's choice of this word is arresting. It conjures up a picture of a person who sees something of interest or importance and, desirous of sharing it with a friend, points to it and says: "Look, share my vision." Is that not precisely what the preacher does who is best at his work? He becomes a pointer.

Here let me quote from a passage in one of the Bishop Martin Memorial Lectures which I gave in 1975, and which I entitled *To be a Pointer* (*On Preaching*, SPCK 1978, pp. 40–41).

There are those who tell us that we should only preach what we know to be true in our own experience. They certainly have a point here. They are in fact appealing for honesty in the pulpit — no high-falutin' phrases, no airy-fairy claim for the faith which won''t stand up to the rigours of human experience, no hot air in homiletics. Good. The point is well made. If I do not personally know the meaning of divine forgiveness, my sermon on that theme will have a hollow ring about it. If I preach eloquently on the peace of God while every line on my face bears witness to a life of acute and obsessive anxiety, then I may have produced a polished essay but I can hardly claim to have *preached* on this theme.

But we cannot leave it at that. For if I preach only what I

109

have experienced, then my hearers will have to live on an impoverished diet. I am not a giant in the things of God, nor indeed are most of us who occupy the pulpits of our churches. Even if we were an Anselm or a Chrysostom, a Luther or a Wesley, a Newman or a Temple, there are limits to one man's experience, and his grasp of truth is bound to be to some extent one-sided. We all have our favourite themes which tend to throw out of proportion the many-sided truth of God. We need others to set our balance right.

Thank God, this is precisely what we have. I am only one, a rather insignificant one, of a great host of men and women who, over long millennia, have known God, loved God, served God, worshipped God, experienced God in far richer and profounder fashion than I am ever likely to do. I am, thank God, part of the one holy catholic and apostolic Church. "The glorious company of the apostles praise thee. The goodly fellowship of the prophets praise thee. The noble army of martyrs praise thee." There are riches here.

So I learn, as a preacher, to become a *pointer*. The great heights of the Canadian Rockies have held for me a kind of alluring fascination since I first saw them in the early forties. I"m not much of a climber. I know something of the exhilaration that comes from the fresh air on the lower slopes. I may even have had a go at a peak or two. Maybe with experience I might climb some of the higher peaks. But there are other men, far greater climbers than I, who have been much higher, ventured far more nobly, and discovered things which I can only faintly guess at. Let me introduce you to them, that in some way at least you may share their experience and catch their vision. That's what the saints are for. That's what the theologians are for. That's what the great explorers, of truth and experience and labour, are for; and even they have never got to the very top of those Rockies of Christian truth. Only One did that, and I want to point to *him* . . .

Yes, I will preach to the limits of my experience of God in Christ. If I have not *something* in that field, I cannot preach at all. But I will preach beyond the limits of my experience. I believe in the one, holy, catholic, and apostolic Church. And I believe in the communion of saints.

We return, briefly, to Manning's definition – "a manifestation of the Incarnate Word, from the Written Word, by the spoken word". "From the Written Word" – Manning is making the point which we underlined in chapters 1 and 3 with quotations from Forsyth and Cranfield to emphasize the central place of the Bible in preaching (see especially p. 77).

The word *homiletics* is currently used in the sense of that department of theology or of theological teaching which has to do with the theory and practice of preaching. But the word is derived from the Greek *homilia* which means "converse" or "dealings with others"; it then came to mean a conversational exposition of a passage or text of Scripture. The scriptural passage or passages having been read (in the synagogue and then, later, in the Christian church), there would be commentary on the text and, very often, conversation by the members of the congregation on that text. Indeed the Church of England in the sixteenth century produced a Book of Homilies for reading in churches to ensure sound doctrine and to make up the deficiencies of clergy who were too unlearned or unskilled effectively to preach. But it was assumed that the subject out of which the exposition and the "converse" emerged was a passage of Scripture.

In the twentieth century, it can by no means always be assumed that the sermon emerges from Scripture (as a rose emerges from a bud). Too often, the *basis* of the sermon is a newspaper article, or a recent publication, or an event of world or local importance. If there is any scriptural content to the sermon, it is more by way of a side reference or a passing glance. If there is a text, too often it is little more than a pretext for the bright ideas of the preacher. When this happens, it is to the great impoverishment of the people who hear (and who, very often, vote by their feet, having found no deep spiritual nourishment in what was given them from the pulpit). What should have been an *illustration* (the newspaper article, the recent publication, the event of the previous week) becomes the *theme*. The Scripture, which should have been the theme, becomes an illustration. The

111

people are not fed. Hungry, they look up; why are they disappointed? Is it because the second clause of Manning's definition has gone unheeded?

Canon Alan Richardson, the late Dean of York, put the matter forcefully when he wrote: "Preaching consists in one thing only: the exposition of the Word of God as contained in the Scriptures in such a way as to bring home its saving and liberating truth to the hearers, enabling them to understand that truth in relation to the situation of their daily lives in the world which Christ came to redeem and which those who are in Christ are called to serve" (*A Dictionary of Christian Theology*, SCM Press 1969, p. 264).

It need scarcely be said that the centrality of Scripture to the act of preaching which we have just emphasized does not imply that every sermon must begin with a text. The announcing of a text (sometimes repeated, with its chapter and verse reference) has often proved to be a sleep-inducing performance. Wise preachers will use a wide variety of ways of beginning a sermon, the better to ensure holding the hearers from the start. But the centrality of Scripture means that the written word will be used to point to the incarnate Word, and that the great doctrinal and ethical themes of Scripture will never be allowed to go by default.

"The written word will be used", we have just said. Yes: but how? It may be desirable to engage in *expository* preaching. The present writer believes that it is, and that for lack of such expository preaching the spiritual life of the faithful is often weak and their ability to communicate the faith is hamstrung. But the fact must be faced that to engage in the steady exposition of the Bible is far more difficult today than it was a few decades ago — and that for at least two reasons.

First, we have to come to terms with the fact of the virtual non-existence of biblical knowledge in the great majority of people who come to church today. We must realize that, in spite of the wide circulation of Bible study notes by such organizations as the Bible Reading Fellowship and the Scripture Union, the Bible is a closed book in the homes of most of our people. Further, the teaching of the Bible in most schools is minimal, in many of them non-existent. The children leave school with little or no knowledge even of the main Bible characters, of the events of Jesus" life, death and resurrection, and of his teaching. Scriptural allusions or quotations found in English literature ring no bells in their minds. A huge gap yawns in their education.

This means that the preacher who wants to take seriously Manning's phrase "from the Written Word" (pp. 196ff) can assume nothing when he attempts the task of expository preaching. Being a man of tact, he will keep that assumption to himself! But he will avoid such a phrase as "the well-known parable of the Rich Fool", and instead will tell that story, vividly, in his own words. Then, and only then, can he begin to do his exposition. This is not "talking down" to the congregation; that is to be avoided at all costs. It is simply coming to terms with the abysmal ignorance of the basics of Christianity in the post-Christian West, as represented in the people in the pews before him.

Secondly, the imagery and thought-forms of the biblical writers differ radically from those with which in everyday life modern people have to do. The contrasts between the simplicities of a pre-Christian and early Christian rural community and the complexities of a modern highly technical and scientific community are immense. Their thought-forms are a hemisphere apart from one another. Sin, blood, propitiation, redemption, sanctification, salvation, eternal life, heaven, hell, the kingdom of God – this is a foreign language to people accustomed to think in terms of modern physics, light-years, word-processors, computers, silicon chips . . . We touch on this again later in this book (p. 153). The point cannot be made too often or too forcefully. How to build a bridge between these entirely different worlds, how to translate the thought-forms and language of the one into those understood by the other, presents the preacher with a task of great proportions, and a challenge which can never be abandoned. Can the work be done without evacuating the old language of at least some of its original content? Can it be simplified without being weakened? "To be simple, you've got to be a great composer", said Dr Alan Wicks, organist of Canterbury Cathedral, in an allusion to the work of Orlando Gibbons. *True* simplicity is the mark, not only of a great musical composer, but of a preacher who has laboured, and never ceases labouring, to bridge the gap between the first century and the twentieth.

＊

So far in this chapter, we have touched on five elements which will have to be included in any attempt at an adequate definition of preaching:

(i)   The personality of the preacher
(ii)   The centrality of Christ
(iii)   The activity of the Spirit
(iv)   The preacher as pointer
(v)   The place of Scripture

There is a sixth element which must be mentioned for inclusion: preaching as an activity of the *Church*, the congregation acting in concert with the preacher. That need only be noted here, for we have elaborated it in an earlier chapter (pp. 79ff).

There is a seventh element which we dare not omit. What is the end in view, the aim, the purpose when we preach? Presumably, we preach in order that things may get done, by the power of God, in the community of God and beyond it. We must give expression to this. Here we may be helped by an ancient and a modern writer.

Augustine put it this way: "*Ita dicere debere eloquentem, ut doceat, ut delectat, ut flectat*" — a speaker should express himself in such a way that he *teaches*, that he *attracts*, that he *turns* (moves the hearer). That is to say, his message must appeal to the whole person, mind (teaching), emotion (attracting), will (turning). That puts purpose in a nutshell.

H.H. Farmer put it this way: Preaching "is God actively probing me, challenging my will, calling on me for decision, offering me his succour, through the only medium which the nature of his purpose permits him to use, the medium of a personal relationship" (*The Servant of the Word*, p. 28). In that definition, Farmer has the advantage over Augustine in that he stresses the fact that preaching is an activity of *God*, but he is at one with Augustine in pointing to the practical aim and purpose of preaching.

There is a passage in the writings of Paul where he deals in some detail with the purpose of preaching. The fourteenth chapter of 1 Corinthians deserves careful study. Paul speaks of *prophesying*, but we may take it in the general sense of an interpretation of God's message, a preaching ministry. He is contrasting it with the gift of tongues. By no means does he despise *glossolalia* – he speaks with tongues "more than you all" (v.18). But if a choice had to be made between these two gifts of the Spirit, there is no doubt which of them he would choose. It would be preaching. His reasons are clear – preaching is intelligible to others and does three things of great value to the Church – it *builds* (edifies), it *stimulates*, it *encourages* (v.3).

It **builds**. The Body metaphor and the Building metaphor were favourites to Paul. He saw preaching as an essential element used by the Spirit in the "bonding together" of the stones of the building (Ephesians 2:21) and the "knitting together" of the limbs of the Body (Ephesians 4:16).

It **stimulates**. When John spoke of the Holy Spirit as the *Paraclete*, he used a word which comes from the same root as the one used here. He is the stimulator Spirit, energizing, suggesting, inspiring, impelling. He is the one at work in the preacher, and the result is the stimulation of mind and conscience. The congregation receives both instruction and encouragement (incitement to action, v.31).

It **comforts**. What congregation, what individual, does not at some time need just that – consolation in grief or depression or distress? As in the ministry of Jesus his programme included the healing of the broken-hearted (Luke 4:18–19), so one of the most important parts of the preaching ministry is the bringing of the deep comfort of the Gospel to those sorely in need of it.

Such preaching is not confined only to the regular members of the congregation. Paul envisages a situation where an unbeliever or an uninstructed person comes under the influence of Christian preaching (1 Corinthians 14:23–25). What happens? God is at work. The man "is convicted and challenged . . . his secrets are exposed" (J.B. Phillips). It is not long before conviction leads to

115

action and he is down on his knees worshipping. He sees that if he is to find God he will find him there — in the Christian congregation. He can halt no longer. He must enter into membership of the Body.

*

In the pages of this chapter we have touched on seven elements any one of which could not be excluded from a definition of preaching without radically impoverishing it. There are, no doubt, other matters which should be included. The writer is half tempted to try to put these ingredients together and produce a definition of his own for the consideration and the critical judgement of the reader. He has decided against doing so. He prefers to suggest that each reader should attempt to do this for himself. Or — and this might be an even more profitable exercise — a group of preachers who have been working together on the subject of preaching might *together* formulate a definition. Or a parish group of preacher and members of the congregation might do the same. When they have reached their result and written it down, let them keep it by them for a year — for two purposes:

(i)   to use it as a test for their own preaching over a period of time;

(ii) to revise and improve it, in the light of further prayer, thought, and practice.

That will prove to be a piece of work of more than academic value.

Grant, O Lord, that
from the written word, and
by our spoken word,
men and women may catch a vision of
the Incarnate Word,
through the power of the Holy Spirit.

"Religion is grace, and ethics is gratitude."

Thomas Erskine

7
Indicatives and Imperatives

"Christians", we have said, "believe in a God who speaks" (p. 31). He spoke, and the worlds were made. He spoke in the Word made flesh, and we beheld his glory. He speaks through his servants down the ages. He is the God who discloses his nature in the deeds he does, in the actions he takes. He is also the God who makes his will known in the commands he gives. He is the God of revelation and of redemption; he is also the God of command and of judgement.

Verbs, so they used to tell us at school, are of various "moods", of which the indicative and the imperative are the most important. **Indicative** verbs make statements. They tell us what happened — in ancient history or last week; what is happening today; what will come to pass tomorrow. They are concerned with reality. They state facts.

Imperative verbs, on the other hand, give orders. They tell us what to do. They are concerned with conduct.

The Christian faith makes use of both moods — indicatives and imperatives — to express the Reality with which it has to do and the conduct expected of those who walk in the Christian Way. This chapter looks at both in the context of the Church's preaching task.

The predominant mood in the Bible is the indicative. That will be a matter of surprise to those who think that the passages which are most meaningful to us are the Ten Commandments (Exodus 20) and the Beatitudes (Matthew 5:3—12). But that is a misconception, however important these two passages are. For being a Christian has much more to it than trying to obey the Ten Commandments, or attempting to live up to the type of character described in the Sermon on the Mount. That is where we go wrong and misunderstand the whole thrust of the Christian faith.

Even in the Old Testament, it is abundantly clear that the indicative, the statement of facts, comes before the imperative, the appeal to conduct. Consider how the story opens: "In the beginning God created . . . God said . . . God saw" (Genesis 1). We are taken, at the very start, into the realm of God's creative activity. Look how the story goes on: Man having got into a mess, the Creator-God proves to be the Redeemer-God and the Sending-God. He says: "I have seen the misery . . . I have heard their cry . . . I have taken heed . . . I have come down . . . I will send you . . . and you shall bring my people out of Egypt" (Exodus 3:7–10). In a sense, there is the Gospel in a nutshell, and the New Testament record is an elaboration of that theme. The Creator-God proves to be the creator of a new society, the Body of Christ, the Church. The Redeemer-God comes down in the Incarnation of Christ. The Sending-God commissions his followers to go into all the world and preach the Gospel, equips them for the task, and goes with them as they pursue it. This can only be expressed in a great swelling series of indicatives – "God so *loved* . . . that he *gave*" (John 3:16); "Christ *died* for our sins . . . *was buried* . . . *was raised* . . . *appeared* . . . " (1 Corinthians 15:3–5); "a sound *came* from heaven . . . and it *filled* all the house . . . " (Acts 2:2); "the church . . . *held* on its way and *grew* in numbers" (Acts 9:31); "he *gave* some, apostles; and some, prophets . . . for the perfecting of the saints" (Ephesians 4:11– 12); "to me, who am less than the least of all God's people, he *has granted* . . . the privilege of proclaiming . . . the good news . . . " (Ephesians 3:8); "I *was* dead and now I *am* alive . . . and I *hold* the keys . . . " (Revelation 1:18).

These great thundering indicatives spring from a God whose character is disclosed by what he *does*. Even the Ten Commandments are prefaced by the indicatives: "God *spoke* . . . 'I *am* the Lord your God who *brought you out* of Egypt' . . . " Behind the imperatives (positive and negative) from Sinai stands the Giver of those commands, who has disclosed himself as a God who cares enough for his creatures to speak to them and who has revealed himself as the Redeemer-God rescuing them from tyranny.

The series of indicatives constitutes a *major* chord. There is nothing minor about them. There is good news in them. God loves his world. God sends men on his saving errands. And — in certain strands of the revelation it is clear — God suffers with his creation. At the heart of the universe, there is a reality which we may dare to call by the title of Father.

With these indicatives as the core of their message, the members of the young Church went to the world with a song in their hearts. The mighty acts of God had been seen in Christ and had resulted in a restored relationship with God; the power of the cross of Christ was a central reality in their faith and experience; the might of the Spirit at work in the Church and through its members in the community bred in them a steady hope and a quiet confidence for this life and the next. God had visited and redeemed his people. Spring was in the air.

Let us turn for a moment from that picture of the Church in the middle of the first century to the Church as we know it in the last quarter of the twentieth. Often, thank God, we can hear the major note in the life and worship of our congregations. Individuals and groups brought up on a stern diet of "thou shalt" and "thou shalt not" wake up to realize the joy of release. God is not a policeman. He is the God of the indicative — who loves, and gives, and comes, and sends, and liberates. That is the Reality at the heart of the universe. Joy to the world! But this is by no means always so in the life of the churches, and the first person to sense it is the preacher. All too often, the members of the congregation whom he addresses are listless, even gloomy. As they direct their look to the pulpit (if indeed they look up there at all!) they seem to say: "What more must we do? What added 'thou shalt' or 'thou shalt not' shall we have to carry away today? Our load is heavy enough already." And then — as the great indicatives of God's re-creating and redeeming love are expounded, the preacher can feel a lifting of the spirit, a sense of relief, a response almost of surprise. "Can *this* be the heart of the faith? It is almost too good to be true!"

The indicatives of what God has done, is doing, and will do bring healing, wholeness, health, holiness; and this not only to the members of the congregation, but to the preacher himself. He realizes that his primary task is not to cajole, not even to exhort, still less to threaten, but to "proclaim the triumphs of him who has called you out of darkness into his marvellous light" (1 Peter 2:9). He is not a little law-giver, urging his people to do good. He is a lover and a pointer (see pp. 109 ff), pointing to him who said: "Come to me, all . . . whose load is heavy, and I will give you relief. Bend your necks to my yoke, and learn from me . . . For my yoke is good to bear, my load is light" (Matthew 11:28–30). He invites his people to explore with him the great doctrines of the catholic faith lest they go by default, and then to relate them to life as it is, in themselves as individuals, in the family, in the local community, in the nation, in the world. His range, and theirs, is as wide as the world. "God loved the world so much . . . "; their love and concern cannot be narrower than his.

All this is so, precisely because Christians are people of the Incarnation. They follow One who was born in a stable, wrestled with the joys and perplexities of boyhood and of adolescence, worked as a tradesman, was hungry, tired and distressed, felt the full force of temptation, died on a cross. The Man of the dirty hands and soiled feet was implicated to the limit in the society of which he was a part and, because he allowed himself to be so implicated, went to his death. "My task is to bear witness to the truth. For this was I born; for this I came into the world . . . " (John 18:37); and such witness, then as now, was costly. It follows that the disciples of the incarnate and crucified Lord are committed to work out, with sweat and tears and, often, with martyrs" blood, the *imperatives* of love. The indicatives of the Gospel lead on inexorably to the imperatives of Christian ethics. Christians can never pull out into a kind of "holy detachment" from the world.

The bearing of all this on the preacher is weighty and demanding.

"I wish you clergy would not interfere in politics or social issues. Stick to your job and preach the Gospel." How often one has heard that said! I recall attending a luncheon in Canada at a time when its Primate, Ted Scott, was deeply involved in relating the Gospel to certain contentious social matters. After the luncheon, which was attended mainly by well-to-do business people, I fell into conversation with one of them and happened to mention my admiration for the Archbishop. "I wish he would not interfere in all these current affairs", said my new friend. I sensed a chilling of the atmosphere. I replied: "His Master did just that, and they crucified him." "Oh, we wouldn't do that", he said.

We cannot avoid it: politics, whether local or central, is the sphere where decisions are made which affect the welfare of society, where things get done which influence for good or ill the development of the young and the welfare of the aged, where grants are made or withheld which lead to the life or death of millions in the so-called third world. God is concerned with housing and drains as well as with human character and destiny. The Christian, just because he is a Christian, must be prepared to get his hands dirty and his feet torn in the world which his God loves and for which his Lord lived and died. You cannot preach the indicatives without going on to expound and apply their implications.

At once we find ourselves in difficulties. Most of us were not trained as politicians, economists or scientists. All too easily, we can make fools of ourselves if we venture into detail in these highly specialist fields. In doing so, we invite (and deserve) the scorn of the experts. What are we to do? We shall do well to be frank with our congregation. We shall not pretend to have pat answers when we have none. We shall seek to enlist their skills and insights in the discussions which will follow our preaching (see chapter 5). But we can go further than this — indeed here is the point where we have our unique contribution to make: We shall seek to elicit from our theological understanding of the Gospel certain broad, basic principles by which ethical actions can be tested. Often we shall find ourselves in areas which are not black or white. There will be big areas of grey where decisions will be difficult, even agonizing. In those areas we must argue and debate and pray and proceed with caution. But the main task of the preacher is to elicit the principles, to point to the guiding lines, to clarify the doctrines, and to stimulate the minds and consciences of his hearers in their applicatory work. If he and his people, in wrestling with some of these problems, sometimes find themselves landed in great doubt and difficulty, well, so be it. They follow One who cried: "My God, my God, why . . . ?" At other times, light will shine from the application of Christian principles to current problems, and shine with such clarity that they will find themselves faced with stark alternatives, and they will have to say: "Here I stand; I can no other." The preacher will have begun his work in clarifying the issues at stake by the truths of the Gospel. He will continue his work by standing in with, and strengthening the hands of, his people as they bear their witness in the market place and pay the price of being disciples of the Crucified.

By way of illustration, let us take one passage which could well be of importance to a thoughtful preacher who does his work in a perplexed society and who seeks to find principles by which to guide its members. The men and women in this preacher's congregation realize that, for good or ill, they live in a world where immense wealth rubs shoulders with abysmal poverty, and where atomic power can be used for beneficial ends or for the extermination of the race. Has the preacher any guidance for them? We shall look at the first of the two creation stories at the opening of the book of Genesis − chapter 1:1−2:4.

On the face of it, it would seem highly unlikely that the men and women of a sophisticated scientific era such as ours would find many directives in a passage of ancient literature such as this. After all, the writer lived in an age which knew nothing of atomic fission, of millions of light-years, of an expanding universe, of the discoveries of an Isaac Newton and still less those of a Fred Hoyle. His concept of our world, let alone of our universe, was almost entirely different from ours. He was no scientist. No; but he was a *theologian*, and he wrote as a theologian. Therein lies the value of his work for us. We look to it, not for what it says or does not say about science or biology, but for what it says about God, about humankind, about nature, about man's enemy, about hope and despair. In fact, it says a great deal, often only touching very briefly on these great issues, but effectively pinpointing central themes which are elaborated elsewhere in Scripture. Gerhard von Rad was right when he said of the first verses of Genesis that they "can hardly be overinterpreted theologically. Indeed, the danger appears greater that the expositor will fall short of discovering the concentrated doctrinal content."

What has the writer to say about GOD?

He does not argue his existence. That was not the Hebrew way. He sees him as the God of *order*, creating a cosmos out of chaos, separating light from darkness, rejoicing in his creation ("God saw that it was good"). Like an artist using his paints, or an author using words, God's creation is there to reflect the mind of the Maker.

He is the *master of time*, as of space. He creates it. He is above it. He does not come under its limitations. He is the Sovereign Lord.

He can best be spoken of in terms of *wind*. The wind of v.2 was not "soft as the breath of even", but an almighty hurricane which swept with creative power over the threatening waters of chaos (the word "swept" is used of the soaring flight of an eagle in Deuteronomy 32:10−12).

He is the God who *speaks*, who desires to communicate with his creation. (see pp. 31ff). To a Hebrew, a word is a powerful thing − "He spake and it was done" (Psalm 33:9).

All this is seminal material. It holds within it the seeds of the fuller revelation which was to come to us in Christ. It suggests a theology closely related to our world and the destiny of those who live in it. This is *God's* world. "The earth is the *Lord's*" (Psalm 24:1). Of this we shall see more in a moment. If man, in his stupidity, were mad enough to blow this world to smithereens and to blot out all life upon it, that would not be the end. God, concerned as he is for his world, is not dependent on it for his continuing existence. He *is*. He will be − whatever happens to our little planet. We may ask whether this note is consistently heard from our pulpits. Are we weak on our eschatology? "If it is for this life only that Christ has given us hope, we of all men are most to be pitied" (1 Corinthians 15:19). Are we affirming this? Or is our message so *this*-worldly-centred that it has no *heavenly* content?

Again, within this passage is the seed of the great doctrine of the divine Logos incarnate in Christ. When John chose "the Word" as the title by which to describe the Christ in the opening chapter of his gospel, his choice owed much more to Genesis 1 than to Greek philosophy, though he chose a word which would have had meaning for both Jew and Gentile. Greek philosophy had much to say about the divine principle of the Logos, but it was Christianity alone which dared to speak of it in terms of a flesh and blood figure in history dwelling among us. John's prologue is the full flowering of Genesis 1. A new creation has been initiated in the Christ event. Genesis 1 is the basis for the whole exposition of God's revelation. And the "mighty wind" can be seen as a foreshadowing of the wind of Pentecost, mighty in the Church and in the world, in conflict with the powers of darkness and chaos.

What has the writer to say about HUMANKIND? ("man", in the generic sense).

He affirms that man-and-woman are made in the "image and likeness" of God. (Two words are used for "image and likeness", but little is gained in trying to distinguish between them.) Perhaps we could say that, as a reflection in a mirror corresponds to the original, so "man" is made in such a way as to reflect some of the characteristics of God. He is so made that something can take place between God and himself. A human being is human in the sense that when God addresses him he can answer. He is a *respons*-ible being in a way that, so far as we know, no other member of the animal world is. Male and female alike share in this divinely-given capacity. Therein lies their equality before God. Neither sexual difference nor colour difference affects this uniqueness. By reason of their being made in the image and likeness of God all members of the human family stand on the same level before God.

This "image and likeness" was not lost at the "fall". It has been marred and defaced but not obliterated. "All have sinned and are falling short of the divine splendour" which God intended should be theirs (Romans 3:23). But they are not outside the reach of redeeming grace, as the New Testament in all its strata is at pains to make clear.

In the heart of this creation story, with its emphasis on mankind made in God's likeness, comes the statement "male and female he created them, God blessed them and said to them, 'Be fruitful and increase . . . ' ". Life as God intends it can only be

128

lived fully if it is lived in community, in communion with God and in communion ("holy communion" as John Robinson used to insist) in the sexual relationship of man with woman. In intercourse between humankind and God and in intercourse between male and female, in community-living at its deepest, is corporate life to be joyfully experienced. The Christian image of God is trinitarian: God is best conceived of as Father, Son and Holy Spirit existing in a community of creative love. This is in some marvellous way reflected in the unity of communion where the great divide of sex is restored in the outworking of God's plan. Here is complementarity at its deepest.

What has the writer to say about "NATURE"?

The God of the first creation story is concerned with sun, moon and stars (what we should call "the universe"; Genesis 1:3ff). He is also concerned with plants, trees, birds, fish and animals (what we should call "nature"; vv.20ff). What is man's position in relation to the God above him and to nature around him? The answer is clear: Man is on this planet as God's vice-regent, his representative, his attorney who administers God's goods. The writer of the book of Wisdom sums it up well: "God of our fathers . . . who hast made all things by thy word, and in thy wisdom hast fashioned man, to be *master* of thy whole creation, and to be *steward* of the world in holiness and righteousness, and to administer justice . . . " (9:1–3). Supreme over nature; accountable to God alone — here is man at his noblest and at his most responsible, exercising authority, but under divine authority himself. He does not own the physical world: he is a tenant within it. The writer of Psalm 8 spells this out magnificently: he looks up at God's heavens in their immensity, the moon and the stars, "set in their place by thee", and asks, "what is man that thou shouldst remember him, mortal man that thou shouldst care for him?" The answer which we might expect is "a mere breath" or "like one of the beasts that perish" — other Psalmists had given these answers (e.g. 104:29 and 49:12, 20). Not so this writer. He replies: "Thou hast made him little less than a god, crowning him with glory and honour. Thou makest him master over all thy creatures; thou hast put everything under his feet." Man is the master of things. Yes: but "*thou* hast made him . . . *thou* hast put everything under his feet." The Psalm ends with: "O Lord our sovereign." The master is subject to the Maker; the creature to the Creator; the tenant to the Owner. In so far as man creates, he is a pro-creator – he does his noblest work on behalf of the Sovereign Lord.

A right relationship with Nature depends on a right relationship with God.

A right ecology springs from a right theology.

What has the writer to say about MAN"S ENEMY?

He has nothing to say about a "fall", a snake, man's disobedience. That is reserved for the second creation story. But behind the first story we can hear a sinister note. The earth was "without form and void". Out of "darkness over the face of the abyss" were born order and light at the bidding of God. Originally, sinister forces reigned, "*but* a mighty wind, a wind of God, swept over the surface of the waters". Behind this creation story lurks the imagery of opposition which recurs in various forms in other parts of the Old Testament – the sea-monster and the many-headed Leviathan (Psalm 74:12ff), the Rahab and the dragon (Isaiah 51:9–10), the floods that lift up their voices and roar (Psalm 93:3–4). Against such forces, the wind and the word of God go to work, and victory is won. This seminal imagery finds its fulfilment in the prologue to John's gospel: "The light shines on in the dark, and the darkness has never mastered it" (v.5). When the Holy Spirit came upon a maid in Galilee and "the power of the Most High overshadowed" her (Luke 1:35), a new creation was born, the beginnings of a new world, a redeemed humanity, "new men, new families, new relationships, new politics", as Karl Barth put it. God's gale did not blow itself out at the creation. It functioned again at Pentecost, "a strong driving wind, which filled the whole house where they were sitting" (Acts 2:2). As Paul put it: "The same God who said, 'Out of darkness let light shine', has caused his light to shine within us, to give the light of revelation – the revelation of the glory of God in the face of Jesus Christ" (2 Corinthians 4:6).

Looking back over this passage, which we have called seminal, we can see how important it *has been* for the development of Christian doctrine. But that is not our primary concern at the moment. We can see how important it *is* for us modern men and women as we seek to wrestle with issues which intimately affect human life and conduct, family relationships, matters of race and sex, ecology, and so on. The Christian approaches these problems with one major question always in his mind: "What sort of God is my God, the God whom I represent in my little sphere of influence within the world he has created and loves?"

The emphasis on "man" as a being who can answer the God who addresses him, a *respons*-ible being, holds within it enormous consequences. What manner of man/woman must he/she be if the image of God is to be reflected? If men and women stand on the same level before God, what has that to say about men's attitude to women, in the home, in the office, in society? Can women be regarded as men's playthings or as their inferiors to be used to their ends? What has it to say in regard to their employment — wages, ordination, and so on? These questions, the outcome of a right theology, will call for a radical alteration in many spheres of life and activity — society, the Church included, has been abysmally slow in applying the implications of Christian theology in this sphere.

The same sort of questions must be asked, and answers demanded, in regard to the race problem, as well as the gender problem. And lest we spend too much time in centring them in South Africa or in Chile (both at a comfortable distance from home), we could make a good beginning in London or Birmingham (if we live in Britain), or in Harlem (if we live in America). Society modelled on the community of the Persons of the Blessed Trinity seems rather far from what we find in modern areas of race riots. It we take seriously the relevance of Christian theology and anthropology, we shall find ourselves asking some very uncomfortable questions, both about race relations and about distinctions of class and privilege.

And man's relation to Nature? What we have outlined above (pp. 129–130) puts in a new light our modern Chernobyls, our pollution of air, of land, of water, our spoiling of natural resources simply to satisfy human greed. This is the *only* light in

131

which they should be seen if God is the Creator and man his procreator, his agent, his tenant. We recall Albert Schweitzer's dominant theme of "reverence for life", and the story of how a friend of his, about to crush a destructive beetle at Lambarene, found a hand laid on his shoulder and heard Schweitzer say: "Gently, Noel! Remember you are a guest in its country." What has this creation story of Genesis 1 to say about the folly — no, the sin — of the arms trade, or about the indifference of the great majority of the people of the West to the warnings of Willy Brandt in his two great reports? What has the Christian conscience, informed by biblical insights, to say to such facts as these: that against a world figure of an arms trade set at $135 billion in 1983, the number of children dying before their fifth birthday was about twenty-eight a minute? Perhaps we should talk a bit less about sorrows, or tragedies, or disasters, and a bit more about sin.

And man's enemy? We should lay more emphasis, surely, on the victory won on Good Friday and Easter Day. And at the same time, we should be more realistic about the powers of darkness still at work. We are not ignorant of the devices of our "enemy the devil, who like a roaring lion, prowls round looking for someone to devour" (1 Peter 5:8). The evidence that the powers of chaos and darkness, the monsters which threaten order and light, are terribly active, is there for all who have eyes to see. The waters of destruction could return and sweep away all that we know as "civilization".

Does this mean that the modern preacher is a prophet of doom? No. He is a realist. He faces facts, and they are grim. He cannot be an easy optimist. He refuses to be escapist. But he is a man of hope — precisely because he is a man of God; and God in the long run cannot and will not be defeated. God has never been the God of the big battalions. He has a way of working through minorities, through "things low and contemptible, mere nothings, to overthrow the existing order" (1 Corinthians 1:28); and he is the God of eternity whose plans will only be completed when time is no more.

The prime duty of the preacher, then, is to think theologically, to view all these issues *sub specie aeternitatis*, and thus to relate the imperatives of Christian ethics to the indicatives of God in Christ, the "ought" of conduct to the "is" of the Gospel. As he does this in his preaching and teaching work, he will, slowly but surely, be enabling those who hear him to look at current problems of ethics as it were through the eyes of God. He will be equipping God's people for work in his service. Then, as they go from sanctuary to market place, they will be able to make their specifically Christian contribution to current debates with a measure, not of cocksureness, but of intelligent confidence.

How often in a discussion on, say, genetic engineering, or abortion, or birth control, the debate focuses on the physical aspect of the problem and hardly at all on the deeper moral and ethical issues of the meaning of person-hood, the sacredness of life, the destiny of the individual, the meaning of the Kingdom of God! The Christian who shares in such a debate has an opportunity to move the discussion to a deeper level; but he can only do so when the preacher has helped him in pulpit and especially in study circle. The power of a Christian contribution, given thoughtfully and springing from deep conviction, can be beyond calculation.

Such a contribution will come as a surprise to many people "in the market place" who had previously thought of Christianity as having to do with a man's private life but having little bearing on social issues. There *is* a kind of so-called Christianity which excessively "privatizes" the Gospel and scarcely relates it to issues social and political; but that will not do. If, as we have seen, our God is concerned with the whole of creation — the universe, "nature", beasts and birds, crops and seasons, men and institutions — his followers must be concerned with no less. All aspects of human activity, all politics, must come under their scrutiny because they are under God's eye. The prophets, as we have seen (chapter 2), found themselves deeply implicated in the politics of their day, and spoke out about them with deep conviction.

We must not fear to follow in their steps, nor must we yield to the temptation to put the clock back and to set limits to human investigation in any sphere of knowledge. In spite of the difficulties in which we shall find ourselves, in spite of the grey areas of doubt, we must never cease to test political and scientific judgement by the acids of theology and make our contribution to the current debates accordingly. Theological understanding is often enriched and extended by new discoveries in other areas of learning. The crucial issue is the testing and the control of knowledge by obedience to the will of God.

To fail in this regard is to invite and to deserve the charge of irrelevancy. The Bishop of Stepney (James Thompson), who has spent twenty years in East London and knows a thing or two about the problems of inner-city work, recently said these wise words in the General Synod of the Church of England: "We are relevant because we have the life-saving relevance of the Gospel that we preach, and the faith, courage and determination of very ordinary Christians and often very suffering and disadvantaged people, who go on believing and having faith in the face of every kind of problem. As long as we bring together black and white to hold and love each other, as long as we transcend middle-class, working-class and non-working-class barriers, as long as the so-called normal and handicapped come together, as long as we create a loving family for the rootless and lonely, as long as we can look at the devastation around us with hope, as long as we call in question the absurd worship of material comfort, as long as we face up to those who say that everything is about money . . . as long as we embrace each other with love and peace, as long as we face the pains and conflicts in the society around us and try with charity to act on them, we shall not be irrelevant."

In that fine statement, the Bishop put his finger on some of the moral imperatives of the Christian faith. To fail to face these imperatives is to do despite to the Gospel and to run away from the path of obedience. No fear of offending his people must shut the mouth of the preacher. It is not for him to tell them what party they are to vote for. It is for him to expose the moral issues involved, to hold them up to the light of the Gospel, and to call for obedience to the Lord of all life from whom alone comes the succour needed for discipleship.

The preacher's stance, which he will seek to share with his hearers, will, first and last, be that outlined by Thomas Erskine and which enshrines the essence of this chapter: "Religion is grace, and ethics is gratitude." The preacher is the servant of both, and spends his life in relating the one to the other.

Spirit of God,
help us who are servants of the word,
so to relate the indicatives of the Gospel
to the imperatives of conscience
that light may shine on the darkness of our ways,
through him who is the light of the world,
Jesus Christ our Lord.

But (when so sad thou canst not sadder)
Cry; and upon thy so sore loss
Shall shine the traffic of Jacob's ladder
Pitched betwixt Heaven and Charing Cross.

Yea, in the night, my Soul, my daughter,
Cry — clinging Heaven by the hems;
And lo, Christ walking on the water
Not of Gennesareth, but Thames!

Francis Thompson: *The Kingdom of God*

8
Eternal and Temporal

The Christian preacher does his work at the point where two worlds meet — the eternal and the temporal. The effectiveness of his ministry may well be measured by his success in rightly relating the two.

If he lives his life and exercises his ministry in the light of his Ordination vows, he is committed to have the main commerce of his life in the things of the spirit and of eternity. If at his Ordination the service of 1662 was used, he will recall that his Bishop charged him and those with him "to be messengers, watchmen, and stewards of the Lord; to teach, and to premonish, to feed and provide for the Lord's family; to seek for Christ's sheep that are dispersed abroad, and for his children who are in the midst of this naughty world, that they may be saved through Christ for ever." The language may be quaint. The intention is perfectly clear. These men are to handle the things of eternity — those things above everything else. The unseen, the eternal, the intangible, but nevertheless, the *real* — God as creator, Christ as redeemer, the Holy Spirit as sanctifier, the Church as the Body of Christ; grace and truth; love, joy, peace; life present and to come; heaven and hell; repentance and faith — these things are the stuff of their ministry, the core of their preaching, the essence of their life and work. Other things matter, and of this we shall have more to say in a moment. But these things are their special care. Other things may be the care of other men; but none other than these for them! They draw all their "cares and studies *this way*". Call them specialists in these things, if you will: they will not mind. Call them narrow, if you will: they mind more about the deeps than the shallows. These things are their glory. They cannot move far from them. They would not if they could.

This, there can be no doubt, is the thrust of the Ordinal; and this is the thrust of the Bible. It is by this thrust that our preaching ministry must be judged. Let a man take out his sermon notes of, say, the last three or four years, and judge them by this thrust — how would they stand the test? The preacher's primary task is to preach about GOD — what kind of picture of him do we draw? A kindly "Daddy" who would not hurt a fly — where is the God of judgement? A Being with whom we can be on terms of hand-shaking familiarity — where is the element of transcendence? We have often heard of the danger of the Christian being so heavenly-minded that he is of no earthly use: is not the present danger of preaching that it is so earthly-centred that it lacks heavenly content? Do we preach about the hereafter? Or is the eternal almost a lost dimension in our thinking and in our teaching? And yet we all, preachers and congregations alike, have to die . . . We say that "our Saviour Jesus Christ has broken the power of death and brought life and immortality to light by the Gospel" (2 Timothy 1:10). No political party will ever proclaim *this*. It is the supreme treasure of the Christian Church — to declare it and to shout it from the housetops. Is *this* our centre of reference?

Dare to look again at those preaching notes. Have we been so absorbed in the present and the temporal, so infected by the passing and the ephemeral, that the element of eternity, of the unseen, has had short shrift or been almost wholly neglected? The Christian preacher is here to deal with time and eternity, and with the things of time in the light of eternity. If he does not do this, then he is presenting a truncated, eviscerated Gospel, if it can be called a Gospel at all. Is it possible we have been preaching "another Gospel which is not another"?

Augustine was right in saying that God made us for himself and that our hearts are restless till they rest in him. It seems clear that many thoughtful people are today turning away from their churches, sick with disappointment because they cannot be sure that in their churches they will have a God-centred pulpit ministry. The human being is made for the truth of God as a baby is made for its mother's milk. There is something within us which refuses to be satisfied if the preacher does not deal with the great realitites of God and man, of sin and grace, of life and death, of time and eternity, of love and justice, of faith and hope. We know we can go elsewhere for discussions on politics and economics. We have a right to look to the Church for a steady exposition of the things which are not seen and yet are eternal. For the preacher to fail his people at this point is to be in danger of his being implicated in treachery.

It will be said that these matters of the spirit, the realities of eternity, are the concern of every committed Christian, not just of the clergy. *Every* Christian must seek to live his life in the light of the conviction that "the things which are seen are temporal; but the things which are not seen are eternal"; the great realities of life are the eternal realities. That is true; and it needs to be said again and again. But the clergy, by their very calling, are to be specialists in teaching theology and in leading worship, and it is as specialists that they do their preaching work.

At this point, where eternal and temporal meet, the preacher finds himself at a point of tension — but it is a tension which can also be a place of power.

As he sits at his desk, immersed in theological thinking, he hears, with the ears of his mind, the cries of the political prisoners in Russia's psychiatric hospitals, of the racially oppressed in Botha's South Africa, of the socially disinherited in Latin America's favellas, of the starving in Ethiopia and the Sudan, of riots in Brixton and Chile, of women assaulted and raped, of children dying for lack of food and medical aid. He sees, with the eyes of his mind, the tragedy of the poor little rich men of the West, possessing all that money can buy and not knowing where to find peace. He reads of the number of suicides, and notes that the rate seems to be highest where scientific sophistication is at its peak. How, in God's name, is he to relate the truths of his theology to the realities which cry out to him from radio and television, from the press, and from the home of Mr and Mrs Jones down the road near his vicarage? Here the two worlds meet. Here is perplexity. Here also is the power of the Gospel.

The truth is that the Christianity with whose exposition the preacher is entrusted, is a this-worldly faith *and* an other-worldly faith, and its glory is only seen to the full when that truth is held in the tension which it presents. One generation may stress the one aspect, another generation the other. But we only get it right (do we ever get it wholly right?) when we stress, and glory in, the tension of the two.

"Jesus knowing that he came from God and went to God" – what is more *other*-worldly, more concerned with the eternal, than that? – "took a towel, and girded himself . . . and began to wash the disciples' feet" – what is more *this*-worldly than that? (John 13:3–5). Jesus got it right. We can only try to follow his example, in our preaching.

We who preach towards the end of the twentieth century have the realities of our world's life and grief more vividly presented to us, and their claims more urgently pressed on us, than any preachers before us. We have the media to thank for that: there it all is in our homes for all of us to see. We have travel to thank for that: we have seen it as we have walked the streets of Soweto or Calcutta or Rio de Janeiro. Is it any wonder that we stress the seen, the temporal, the tangible realities of life? We are right to do so. But not, please not, at the expense of the eternal. It is all too easy for the Christian preacher to become little more than a political commentator – and that is total tragedy.

What, then, is he to do? He must be a realist. He must know what is going on in the world – in his parish and in China! In one hand he will have his Bible: in the other his daily newspaper. It is his task – what a task! – to link the two. And if he feels that that part of his calling is impossible, let him remember that the prophets and Our Lord himself did it before him.

The Jewish prophets did their work from the midst of a political maelstrom. Their little country was set at the point where the great highways met and the great civilizations passed through. The prophets were men with a strong political bent, deeply concerned with the rise and fall of nations and with the welfare of their tiny people as one civilization flourished and another fell into decline. And they were men with a powerful social emphasis. No language could be too strong for their condemnation of oppression of the poor by the rich, of the crooked business deal, of the blasphemy of religious services when those who participated in them were living immoral lives. But their *prime* theme was GOD, the God of justice and judgement, the God of love and mercy, himself deeply concerned about and implicated in the issues of the day. The prophets did not prophesy by talking about politics and then adding a touch of God-talk, appending a religious gloss to some fashionable line of current secular thought. They prophesied about God and viewed history and moral conduct in the light of his Being and activity.

Jesus himself followed in their steps. In his first sermon at Nazareth, he took the words of Isaiah 61 and made them the charter for his own ministry just about to begin. It was to be a ministry to "the poor, the prisoners, the blind, the broken victims" of society. The stories in the gospels bid us take those words literally — these unfortunates, these social outcasts, were the people closest to the heart of Jesus, and to them he ministered. That was an integral part of his Gospel. But let us not put a full-stop where the record only puts a comma — " . . . to let the broken victims go free, *to proclaim the year of the Lord's favour*" (Luke 4:18—19). In that last phrase is the climax of it all — God's clock had struck: the Reign of God had arrived in the Person of the preacher; repent; believe the Gospel. A similar balance is found in a fine summary of the purpose of the coming of our Lord in Mark (10:45): "The Son of Man did not come to be served but to serve" — what better delineation of the social service to Jesus' ministry could there be than that? But that is not all: he came "to give up his life as a ransom for many". In those seemingly simple words we are taken into the heart of the Eternal, into the unseen things of sin and forgiveness which are the real things, the stuff of which life — and preaching — are made.

The preacher seeks to follow in the steps of the prophets and of Jesus. His first concern is "the Kingdom of God and his righteousness", the Reign of God and his justice. God is King and God is Father. That is the basic eternal truth, and by it all ethical decisions, all political programmes, must be judged. The preacher is an "assayer" in the sense that, when he speaks of moral and ethical issues, he seeks to submit them to analysis in the light of eternity: how much true metal, and how much dross, is there in this or that policy if it be tested thus? The preacher is in the pulpit not to curry votes for a political party. He is there to do something much more profound and much more difficult — to measure issues of human justice, of class or gender discrimination, of sexual ethics, of ecological responsibility, by the plumbline of the vision of God as Father, King, and Judge. He is there to elicit principles and then to expound them in relation to the issues of the day. If God is the God and Father of our Lord Jesus Christ; if men and women, whatever their class or colour, are made in the image of God and are children of eternity; if the world is of God's creation and is entrusted to the care of human beings; if sin is a reality and deliverance from it a glorious fact; if all these things (which are the stuff of his regular preaching) are so, then let them be the decisive factors in the light of which contemporary issues are judged, decisions made, votes cast. Sometimes the decisions called for will be clear — the strong light of the Christian Gospel shows up the wrongs and rights of a particular situation and there can be little doubt what the disciple's answer must be. Often the areas are grey; and prayer, thought, and debate are called for in the application of principles to current issues. That process may be long and agonizing. That is part of the cost of discipleship. But it can also prove to be a means of growth to the preacher himself and to those whom he serves in pulpit, in discussion group, and in the casual intercourse of every day. In refusing to give pat answers, in pushing back behind the questions to eternal principles, he will be following the example of Jesus himself, and will encourage the only kind of growth worth having, growth in truth reached the hard way. The preacher is above all else the man of theology, the man of religion, there in the pulpit to show that a sound ethic can only proceed from a sound theology, and that right decisions, in the political and social spheres, can issue only from right religious and moral principles.

Does that mean that the preacher cannot be specific in his application of such principles to particular situations, be they international or local? Not at all. The Incarnation was very "specific" — it had to do with a Person born in a stable, working at a bench, his hands dirty and his feet thorn-pierced, his body crucified . . . God is concerned with the specific — with a working man's wages, a child's health, the nature of housing and education, illiteracy, prostitution, drugs, life as it is in its glory and its crudity and its profanation. This God is our God. Our concerns can be no other than his. To say that is to enter the world of politics, for politics has to do with the relationships of men in society; it is the area where decisions are made which affect the welfare of nations and men. How often we hear it said: "I wish you preachers would keep politics out of the pulpit!" Sometimes the reason for such a remark is that the preacher is little more than a political commentator who adds a dash of religion to his weekly essay. In that case, we sympathize with the complainant. We have already in this chapter dealt with this approach. But all too often the complaint springs from the fact that the preaching has got too near the bone to be comfortable to the hearer: "theory", as he would call theology, has implications too closely related to human relationships, to bank balance, to ballot box! Martin Luther King, Janani Luwum, Oscar Romero, Maximilian Kolbe and thousands of others in this century alone, have witnessed to the impossibility of divorcing religion and politics, if they were to be faithful to the Lord whom they served. They have witnessed to the death. All Christians are called to be "martyrs" (the word simply means witnesses), some, like those just mentioned, witnessing by their deaths, all witnessing by their lives and their lips.

The preacher who fulfils his calling in the way we have indicated in this chapter will be accused of "interfering" – "let the cobbler stick to his last, the preacher to 'religion' ". The accusation only points to a total misunderstanding of the Christian religion on the part of the accuser. The Christian's God has made himself known by his "interference" in the world of men and women – supremely at the "interference points" of Bethlehem and Calvary. Here the eternal penetrates the temporal. From that penetrating interference the Faith draws its power. At that point, it makes its costliest demand.

Lord God,
the protector of all who trust in you,
without whom nothing is strong, nothing is holy:
increase and multiply upon us your mercy,
that you being our ruler and guide,
we may so pass through things temporal
that we finally lose not the things eternal.
Grant this, heavenly Father,
for the sake of Jesus Christ our Lord.

Ubi caritas, deus ibi est

9
Charity and Clarity

"It is for love of him that I do not spare myself in preaching him." The words are those of Gregory the Great who sent Augustine on his mission to England. They come in one of Gregory's sermons in which he was preaching about Ezekiel as a watchman of the Lord and comparing his own ministry with that of the prophet. He spoke of his own unworthiness, and then went on: "And yet the creator and redeemer of mankind can give me, unworthy though I be, the grace to see life whole and power to speak effectively of it." And then the words in which with powerful simplicity he put his finger on the very heart of all preaching: "*It is for love of him* that I do not spare myself in preaching him."

"For *love* of *him*." *Caritas* was the word he used. It is a pity that we cannot use the English word "charity" without danger of being misunderstood. In Gregory's day, and indeed for centuries after him, it was the strong, un-sentimental, muscular word for love; only in comparatively recent centuries has it become enfeebled, till now it is often used in the limited sense of a gift given by a more liberally endowed member of society to a less fortunate one. But *caritas* has a depth to it and a strength to it which reflects something of its Greek equivalent, *agapé*; and because of this I have kept it in the title of this chapter.

"It is for love of him." Gregory is saying that he preaches, and does so without caring what it costs him, simply because he loves God. Perhaps a very human analogy might throw light on what Gregory was getting at. A man falls in love; for him there is no one like the girl he has met and intends to marry. It will come to him as something of a surprise to notice how often he wants to introduce his fiancée to his friends — "I want you to meet her", he says again and again. It is for love of her that he introduces

149

her. Is this an over-simplification of what Gregory is talking about? Of course it is. But there is enough truth in it to get us thinking. Is *caritas*, love of God, the motive, driving force behind our preaching? Perhaps in the earlier days of our service of God, the emotional element played a bigger part than it does in later years. That matters little. Love has emotion as one of its constituents, and it is an important constituent. But the volitional, and the moral, and the intelligent constituents within love are deeper, more abiding, more important. All these go into the making of our love for God. And it is for such "love of him that I do not spare myself in preaching him".

The preacher's love for God is the result of his realizing that he is a man infinitely in debt. "Thanks be to God for his gift beyond words" (2 Corinthians 9:15). He can never repay that debt. But because he knows that he is in debt to Christ, his preaching becomes something of a passion. He begins to understand what Paul meant when he wrote: "I passionately hope I . . . shall speak so boldly that now as always the greatness of Christ will shine out clearly in my person" (Philippians 1:20).

This love of God — God's love for him and his return-love to God — is a formative power in the preacher himself; we might dare to say, a transforming power. The preacher, if he is really to preach, must himself be constantly, and until death, "in process of formation". We recall the words of the American preacher, Quayle: "Preaching is the art of making a sermon and delivering it. Why no! Preaching is the art of making a preacher and delivering that." A great Jew, Leo Baeck, wrote: "A message is not the preaching of a preacher, but rather the man himself. He is the decisive element; only if he himself is a message can he bring a message. For only then will there go forth from him that reality which is conveyed in Dante's sentence: 'he speaks reality, and you speak words'. In the last analysis, therefore, only a pious man can preach." The point is taken. "What you are speaks so loud that I cannot hear what you say" — that is not just the clever quip of a cynic; it enshrines a great truth. And only the love of God — poured out in Christ and responded to by ourselves — can make us into preachers. "It is for love of him that I do not spare myself in preaching him."

150

Such love for God overflows. "Flooding our inmost heart through the Holy Spirit he has given us" (Romans 5:5), it overflows in a great compassion for others. As a result, we could venture to alter one word in Gregory's great sentence and, in a secondary sense, say: "It is for love of *them* that I do not spare myself in preaching him." This was the motive power behind the teaching-and-preaching ministry of Jesus. When he saw a great crowd, so Mark records, "his heart went out to them" — *there* was *caritas*! — and he set about teaching them (6:34). "When a crowd gathered round him once again, he followed his usual practice and taught them" (10:1). That teaching-preaching work was an outflow of his compassion, an outflow of the love of God within him. No wonder people noted his authority — it was the authority of a divine compassion.

John Killinger puts this well: "The preacher's first calling . . . is to love. Otherwise the preacher doesn"t understand community and has nothing to preach. We must love the community and love the people who belong to the community. It is not enough, if one wishes to preach, to be in love with preaching. It is not enough . . . to be in love with the Christian philosophy. It is not even enough to be in love with God. We must love people and love God's vision of the community. Then we can preach" (*Fundamentals of Preaching*, SCM Press, 1985, p. 8).

This will mean that we never harangue our hearers, as it were "from above". There will not be much denunciation of "you sinners". There will be much more of "we" than of "you". We are in the bundle of life together with them — all of us sinners in need of the grace of God; all of us together on the road to eternity. As we preach like this, they will know that we love them.

So far in this chapter, then, it looks as if preaching is essentially a love-affair — the preacher in love with his God and in love with his people. Is it possible or right, then, in any sense to speak of preaching, as many have done, as an *art*? *The Art of Preaching* — that was the title of a well-known book by Charles Smyth, published in 1953. The phrase flashes a red warning-light in my mind at once. It is like calling the sacred ministry a "profession".

Our hackles rise — and rightly. It is so much more — it is a calling; it has about it a touch of divine summons and human response, of the numinous and the eternal. A profession? Yes: but only if in the same breath we add "and so much more". Having said that, the clerk in Holy Orders *is* a professional and his people have the right to expect of him all the marks of expertise, of conduct and of bearing which belong to a man trained and set aside for this particular work. So of preaching. An "art"? Yes: and so much more.

But an art it is. Call it a craft if you will — Dr W.E. Sangster wrote a book called *The Craft of Sermon Illustration* (1946) and another *The Craft of Sermon Construction* (1949). It is a strategy, in the sense in which the headmaster of a school defined teaching as "the strategy by which we help the child to develop".

Art — craft — strategy: we need not fear the words. After all, Christian disciples are described in the New Testament as fishermen, shepherds, scholars; and all of these spheres of activity call for highly developed skills and the harnessing of hard-come-by knowledge to the end in view. As I use these words in connection with preaching, my mind conjures up pictures of sleeves rolled up, wet towels, ample wastepaper baskets, dictionaries well-worn, books loved and used; a carpenter cares about his tools.

All the tricks of the trade, all the rhetoric in the world, will not make a sermon. The Gospel is concerned with throwing a lifeline to drowning men — that is one aspect of preaching. But in the throwing, *skill* and *expertise* are called for.

"The art of preaching" has implications which must be taken seriously. The first implication is the avoidance of jargon, and here great skill is called for. This presents us with real problems. Jargon is defined as "specialized language concerned with a particular subject, culture or profession". The preacher of the Christian Gospel is handling theology, and theology has a language of its own which he has been trained to understand. To him it is meaningful. But to most of his people it is not, at least until he has done a good deal of preparatory teaching work. He must never cease to wrestle with the task of breaking down the specialized language of theology without in the process evacuating that theology of its essential content. The point is worth pursuing.

In May 1985 the leaders of thirty-two Churches in England, Scotland and Wales met and agreed to launch a three-year Inter-Church Process of prayer, reflection and debate together on the nature and purpose of the Church in the light of its mission. They were determined to listen to what the people in the pews were thinking and saying. In Lent 1986, about one million people took part in a series of discussions by means of radio, cassettes and meetings. Some sixty to seventy thousand groups met. Most sent in a report on their findings. In addition, some hundred thousand people returned individual completed questionnaires.

A trained group set to work to process the material. As a result, a small book, *Views from the Pews*, was published by the British Council of Churches in the autumn of 1986. This unique book enables us to hear, not the views of church leaders, but what the ordinary lay men and women think.

Two things relevant to our theme emerge clearly, and they are closely related. The *first* is that *"Jesus is hidden by the jargon"*. "There is still a great deal of archaic (and therefore unintelligible) terminology used in churches . . . It was strongly recommended that such language should be replaced by contemporary words and the modern idiom." "Because of this 'blockage' it was evident that some of the most important teachings of basic Christian doctrine were appreciated, at best, only very imperfectly." "Theology has come to be regarded as a mystery which can be unravelled only by experts, and therefore the average members of the Church are not expected to have any theological insights . . . " In answer to a question as to what people think the local church should be doing, the top option was "helping people to pray". A very close second was "teaching the Faith".

The *second* thing which emerged was this: "People were asking for help with evangelizing or outreach, but *seemed to be afraid to share their faith*." Why this fear? Is it not the direct result of lack of teaching on the part of those who are supposed to be competent to give that teaching, namely, the clergy? More

THE SACRAMENT OF THE WORD

and more the task of the clergy is seen to be that of *enablers*, there "to equip God's people for work in his service" (Ephesians 4:12). If they are not solidly and systematically teaching the Faith, is it to be wondered at that the mouths of God's people are shut for fear that they should "get it wrong" when they are in dialogue with opponents of the Faith or those perplexed about it? To put the matter more positively: the members of a well-taught community are likely to be the people most success-ful at outreach.

The avoidance of jargon is *not* a plea for less theology in the pulpit. It points to the need for more theology, but theology cluttered with fewer technical terms, more suited for comprehen-sion by those who, not technically trained, want to take their part, in home and market place, in the spread of the Gospel. One is tempted to misquote Paul, for the misquotation is pointedly true: "though I speak with the tongues of men and of angels, and have not *clarity* . . . I am nothing." There can be no clarity unless and until we work at the language we use and at the avoidance of jargon.

Further, the choice of the English we use, our actual vocabul-ary, should be worthy of the truth we seek to convey. Dr Kenneth Slack, writing of that fine ecumenical figure Norman Goodall, said: "The character of his speech . . . was not merely an external thing: it was sacramental of this man's faith. If he had to speak of this faith, or of the life of the church which enshrines it, it was natural for him to enshrine what he had to say . . . in the beauty which he believed to be one of the attributes and manifestations of God." When you give your wife a pearl necklace, you do not wrap it up in newspaper.

If clarity of content is important, clarity of *aim* is scarcely less so. The river Meander is, as I recall it, a pleasant and harmless little stream in Turkey. It wanders on its way. It looks pretty, but it does not appear to get much done. One certainly could not harness any energy from it. It has given its name to the verb "meander" which the dictionary defines thus: "To follow a winding course; to wander without definite aim or direction." That is an apt, a cruelly apt, description of much preaching. While the river Meander, to all appearances, does not seem to know where it is going, the river Niagara shows every evidence of having a purpose in view — to get over those Falls as quickly as it possibly can. Therein lies its power — waiting to be harnessed and so to give light to millions.

It would be a godly discipline for us to ask each sermon, before we preach it: "What is your purpose? What one thing are you trying to say and to achieve?" If we cannot answer that question briefly, and preferably in monosyllables, it may point to there being something wrong with that sermon. Or let us put it another way: "What am I asking the Holy Spirit, the Lord, the Life-giver, to *do* through the preaching of that sermon?" The story is told of a theological student who wrote out a sermon for his homilectics teacher, and read it to him. A long silence ensued, and the student sensed that there was something ominous about it. At last, he could wait no longer: "Will it do, sir?", he said, "will it do?" "*Do what*?", was the reply.

Sometimes the reason for a sermon being Meander-like is that the preacher has packed too much into it. Stand back and look at that sermon and it resembles nothing so much as the window of some great general store, packed, every inch of it, with goods. Any impression left on the mind of a viewer is that of lots of bits and pieces, but nothing more. But go to Bond Street in the West End of London or to Fifth Avenue in New York, and the picture is entirely different. There, in the centre of the window, against perhaps a black background, is one precious object. All the lights are focused on that alone. It is an invitation to you to break the commandment and to covet! Subtly, but so powerfully, it says: "Look at me. Get me. Buy me. *I am the one thing that you must have.*"

"This one thing I do" — every sermon should be able to say just that.

Clarity of **diction**. One is inclined to apologize for mentioning this, but experience emphasizes the need of doing so. It is surprising to see the use of amplifying apparatus in some quite small churches. Apart from the bad aesthetic effect of some of this apparatus and the frequent breakdown of it in use, there is no need for it at all if the one apparatus with which we all are endowed — the human voice — is properly used. The question at issue is not one of volume but of clarity.

There is no need to shout, even in a big building. But there is imperative need for clear diction and for remembering elementary rules such as refraining from dropping the voice at the end of sentences. Each of us is given a voice with the possibility of wide range within it; if we get into the habit of using only a fraction of that range, it is scarcely to be wondered at if the congregation drops off to sleep — what is more soporific than monotony? Use the range of voice with which God has endowed us, and the interest of our hearers will be maintained and stimulated.

Most of us, especially those who live or work in the big conurbations, are bombarded with noise — aeroplanes, lorries, radios, television, shouting ... It is likely that our hearing apparatus is damaged by this constant assault on its delicate mechanism. All the greater need, therefore, for that clarity of diction which will relieve people from the burden of straining to hear the words of the preacher; most will give up after a brief struggle, and then even the words of a golden-mouthed Chrysostom will be useless!

There is no excuse for the twentieth-century preacher to fail in the matter of diction. There are plenty of experts to help him. And if he has no access to such personal assistance, let him make a recording of himself at work and then submit that recording to rigorous judgement. We can learn from our faults. "Oh wad some power the giftie gie us" to hear ourselves as others hear us! That power is ours in modern electrical recording systems.

Clarity of **presentation**. In judging the culinary art, marks are given for "presentation". Of course the contents of the dish matter — is it nourishing? But the presentation of the dish before the eater matters also — the food must not be thrown at him anyhow. There should be an element of seemliness, even of beauty, in the way in which it is served. It must look appetizing. So with preaching.

In the next chapter we shall consider the value of **silence**, before, after, and even during the sermon. Was it not Mozart who said: "The rests are more important than the tune!"? Have pity on the listener and give him a rest from your voice. Let the

Holy Spirit register the truth of what he has said through you. He can do that best in the silence.

What about **humour**? Take a leaf out of Shakespeare's book. He knew the wisdom of bringing the fool on the stage from time to time: the audience needed relief from the pressure of high drama; laughter would provide it. The masters of music, too, know that a short and quiet piece slipped in between the massive movements of a sonata not merely soothes the listeners but prepares them for what is to follow. A touch of humour, providing it is relevant to the subject in hand, gives a rest, a kind of breathing space, to the congregation. I love to watch a ripple of amusement pass over a congregation, or even to hear a full-bellied laugh – why do we make a religion with joy at its heart so solemn?

Beginnings and **endings** are of crucial importance. If the beginning is dull, we shall lose our people's attention and it will be very difficult to recapture it. If the ending is dull, we may undo the work which the sermon aimed to carry out. Specially careful preparation, therefore, is called for. As we work at the beginning of the sermon, we say: "Don't lose them (the congregation." As we work at the ending, we say: 'Don't waste it (the sermon)."

The ending presents us with special temptations. By the time we have got there in our preparation, we are tired and tend to leave it to the inspiration of the moment – an inspiration which rarely comes. As a result, the sermon trails off into nothingness or a few pious platitudes. How much better to have a short resumé of what has been said, a quick final tap of the trowel on the brickwork, and then – silence. "He's done, but he winna finish" was the criticism made by a shrewd Scotsman of a preacher and the sermon he had preached.

We are told that ours is not a listening age, and that people have largely lost the ability to concentrate for any considerable length of time. That is true. We are accustomed to headlines and snippets of news, its and bits of gossip, not to lectures which call for lengthy attention. Moreover, most sermons – not all – have no visual aids; thus an extra burden is placed upon the preacher. All this must be borne in mind. Except in the case of congregations very well trained, or of preachers with very special gifts, it may well be wise not often to exceed the fifteen-minute mark within, for example, a service of Holy Communion. But this in itself presents a special challenge to the preacher, for the simple reason that a short sermon calls for more preparation than does one which meanders on. The Duke of Wellington apologized for the length of his despatches from Spain — "I had not time to make them shorter."

This is no excuse for sermons which are little more than snippets — the whole tenor of this book has refuted any such suggestion. It is simply a plea for facing the realities of the situation as it is today. If we learn the art of using to the full a fifteen- or twenty-minute period for most of our preaching work, we may be surprised to find how much solid teaching can be accomplished in that time. And we may find — or make — other occasions when lectures can be given, say during a weekday course or a teaching mission, to meet the needs of those who want to enter more fully into the riches of our inheritance in the Christian faith.

Grant, O God,
that I may speak so boldly
and so lovingly
that the greatness of Christ
may shine out clearly in my person,
through the indwelling of your Holy Spirit.

Silence in public worship "is an appropriate way of receiving the word of God — a restful waiting upon God, detached from outward distractions and receptive to the influence of divine grace."

A Companion to the Alternative Service Book 1980: (R.C.D. Jasper and Paul F. Bradshaw, SPCK 1986, p. 104)

10
The Power of Silence

Why should there be a chapter on silence in a book on preaching? Preaching has to do with words; and words, in the nature of the case, make noise. That is true. But *the efficacy of the words spoken depends* in large part *on the silence out of which they proceed*.

At this point, the preacher needs to do some hard thinking for himself, in relation to his personal pattern of life and conduct. And he needs to undertake a very considerable teaching operation as the leader of the worship in which he and his people share. If he is wise, he will find himself returning to this matter frequently over the years.

He himself and the people of his congregation live in a world of noise. Even if that be a platitude, a glimpse of the obvious, it needs to be faced. The busy-ness and noise of the cities have invaded the one-time peace even of our country villages — the noise of lorries and cars, the blare of radio and televison. Human beings are the target of a constant bombardment of sound, often blaring, often cacophonous. In many homes, the radio or television is more or less permanently switched on, and conversation has to be conducted against a background of noise half listened to and half resented. Without their realizing it, the victims of this noise are subjected to strains which in the process of time may well lead to tension, irritability or nervous breakdown. Even cyclists can be seen with headphones clamped to their ears (to the danger of other travellers), and walkers, similarly equipped, shut out the lovely sounds of nature. It would be an interesting exercise to search out the reason for modern man's apparent desire for noise, to define why he feels that almost every moment must be filled with sound. Is he *afraid* of silence? And if so, why?

But there are many who, in a world of noise, long for silence. The popularity of our cathedrals may be evidence of such a search (though even in our cathedrals the sheer number of visitors militates against the success of that search). The fact that our Retreat houses are full to overflowing may indicate a desire to flee from noise and to enter into quiet even if only for a few hours or, at best, a few days. If the Church does not give a lead at this point of human need, who else will? Where shall silence be found? Where, if not in our churches?

In this connection, we should do well to sit at the feet of those who have gone before us, and not least to listen to the old Hebrew seers, prophets and, especially, psalmists. "The Lord is in his holy temple; let all the earth be hushed in his presence." Habakkuk (2:20) uttered those words long before the beginning of the Christian era. We should carefully attend to them late in its twentieth century.

The Hebrews had a word for it, *tiqwah*. It is a rich word. It holds within it the various ideas of hoping, waiting for, depending on, looking to. It presupposes that the Object of such quiet activity is One who can be wholly relied on for strength, deliverance, refreshment. (Typical passages are Psalms 37:9; 40:1; 130:5; Isaiah 25:9; 40:31.) "Hope" to a Hebrew meant far more than it does to a modern when he uses such a phrase as "I hope it will be fine tomorrow" or, sarcastically, "What a hope!" To an Old Testament man of religion, it meant a steady confidence in a God who, having entered into a covenant relationship with his people, would never break it. Such a hope, derived from and strengthened by waiting quietly on God, gave an unshakeable basis to life. It steadied. It nerved. It held. It was the antidote to the hectic activism which so often leads to breakdown. It was the secret of endurance. It was the answer to despair. Men and women imbued with such a hope "will win new strength, they will grow wings like eagles; they will run and not be weary; they will march on and never grow faint."

"All my hope on God is founded;
He doth still my trust renew"

– that is good Old Testament religion. It is even better New Testament experience.

The silence of which we speak is not merely the absence of noise. That absence is important and has to be planned and worked for. But silence is recollection, or, better, re-collection: the collecting together of a man's distraught self, his thoughts and desires, his sins and lusts, his hopes and fears, his ambitions and disappointments, in the presence of him who said: "Come unto me, and I will give you rest."

Further, in terms of a congregation, it is the collecting together of isolated individuals into a corporate body of people who have one object in view, namely, the worship of Almighty God. The word "congregation" means by derivation the collecting together of a flock (Latin *grex*, *gregis*). We have all seen a field with a hundred sheep, each intent on its individual nibbling. We come to church rather like that, each an individual with our own interests and desires. But in worship, we become a flock, a congregation, a body intent on a purpose, the offering of worship. Our exaggerated individualism gives way, for a brief hour at least, to a corporate activity of immense significance.

This is not easy of achievement. Let us be very practical at this point. So far as the preacher is concerned, the task of achieving silence in the worship on Sunday begins at his prayer-desk and in his study during the week. That is easier to write than to work out. To examine the diary of many clergy is to engage in a study of perpetual motion. Nor are the clergy entirely to be blamed for this. If you are in charge of a parish of thirty thousand people and have an inadequate staff (or none at all), or if you have five little villages each an entity in itself and each refusing to do anything with any other of the villages, can you wonder if the life of the parish priest is one long whirl of activity, and that there is more of perspiration than of inspiration in what he does and says? Let us cast a kindly eye on this man of motion.

But at the same time, this must be said in charity even if it sounds cruel: We find time, or make it, for the things which, in our deepest conviction, we deem to matter most. If we really know what preaching is, and if we believe it to be of primary importance to do it well, we shall make time for that prayer-desk

165

and study-desk which are basic necessities to the fulfilling of a preaching ministry. If there is no centre of quiet to the storm of activity which rages round the preacher, he will bring to his conduct of worship, including that part of it which is preaching, a sense of his own turmoil and restlessness which cannot but be felt and shared by the members of the congregation. This is a subtle matter, but none the less real for that. The spirit which dominates the preacher communicates itself to the members of the congregation. The preacher must, therefore, fight to maintain his life of prayer and his time for reading, study, and preparation. There are no short cuts in this area. In his contacts with people during the week, he will learn of their needs. In his contact with God each day of the week, he will learn how to meet those needs.

It is a tragedy when a preacher is found to have abandoned the battle for serious reading. His preaching will reflect that abandonment as surely as will a concert pianist's performance reflect his abandonment of practising. It will be thin and watery, repetitive, and narrow in the sweep of its range. It will be lacking in nourishment.

There is unlikely to be release from this battle for a right place for serious study in the preacher's diary. But at least let the battle be joined! And let the preacher's prayer constantly be something like this: "Lord, teach me that I may teach them. Let my mind be alert, enquiring, searching. Save me from mental rust."

From prayer-desk and study, the preacher moves to the vestry of his church. This is the ante-room of the sanctuary. Those who gather there, assistants, choir members, church wardens, must learn that here, well before they move into the church, all talking ceases. The period of total silence may be short, even only one full minute, but the silence must be total. Then comes the briefest prayer uttered by priest or lay person. Thus prepared, the people in the vestry carry with them into church a spirit of stillness, a sense of re-collectedness, which infects the members of the congregation to their great good. It may take some time and a good deal of patience to teach this to those concerned, but the efficacy of the lesson once learned will be powerful.

Next, the people in the pew must be taught the need for preparatory silence. Experience suggests that there will always be some who arrive just as the service begins, or even after it has begun. But if the majority of the congregation has learned that the five minutes before the beginning of the service hold within them a large part of the secret of success of what is to follow, even the late-comers will find it easier to worship. What are these people doing? They are re-collecting themselves. They are becoming a unity bent on worship. They are focusing on God, "homing in" on God. The next sixty minutes are going to be the most important hour of the week — how shall it be spent? They must say a prayer not only for themselves but for him or her who will be leading the service; for those who will be taking some public part in it; for the preacher with whom they will be working when the time for the sermon arrives. Those five minutes, rightly used, will be creative.

The service, thus prepared for in the vestry and in the body of the church, begins. Too often, no provision is made for periods of silence during the hour that follows — some sound is going on all the time. To allow this to happen is to miss a major opportunity. There is healing in silence intelligently explained and properly used. However dulcet the tones of the man in charge, the congregation will appreciate a little rest from time to time. Let him give way so that, out of the silence, the voice of God may be heard, the voice that is not heard in the great and strong wind, nor in the earthquake, nor in the fire, but in the sound of a gentle stillness (1 Kings 19:11–12). For example, after the reading of each lection, silence should be kept so that the words of Scripture may register their message. The prayers offer a golden opportunity for silent praise or intercession — and so on. A congregation unaccustomed to such pauses in the flow of sound will have to be introduced to them slowly. But the benefit of such periods of silence will soon be felt.

Now comes the sermon. The preacher enters the pulpit. The reading of the Gospel (or the creed or the hymn) ends. This is a critical moment. The briefest prayer or invocation and the congregation sits. What then? This is the point where there is every possibility of the congregation disintegrating — not physically, of course, but in the sense that they cease to be a congregation and relapse into being a hundred individuals, the thoughts of each member wandering. The businessman thinks: "Did I make a right investment on the Stock Exchange last week?" The mother: "Did I peel enough potatoes for the family meal?" The daughter: "Will Granny be all right till I get back?" And the weary: "Can I get a few minutes' sleep before the next hymn?" *This* is the moment when the preacher re-collects the flock. Lose them at this moment, and it will be a task of mammoth proportions to win them back again. This is the point where silence is at its most potent. Wait. Wait till they have settled. Wait till they have put their books down. Wait till their eyes are turned to the pulpit. Wait, if necessary, till they wonder why the sermon has not started: is the preacher ill? Then, only then, begin.

During the sermon — silence *then*? Surely not! Surely *yes*! The power of pause is immense. I watched an entertainer recently on television. He was engaging in a piece of buffoonery. But I learnt two things from those few minutes of performance — the power of clear diction, and *the power of pause*. Actors call it timing. That is helpful. I attended a lecture not long ago. The lecturer was well qualified; he knew his subject and was widely read in it. The matter was good and there was plenty of it. But there were practically no pauses; for fifty minutes we were at the receiving end of a never-ceasing stream of words. But did we receive? It was a bombardment. But did the bombs reach their target? It was a tap flowing at full speed. But could our containers take it? Most of us, I think, gave up in a state of mental exhaustion. It was a pity, for good material was going to waste.

In pleading for pauses, I am not asking the preacher to engage in some rare form of rhetoric or to achieve some startling histrionic effect. I am asking him to put into operation a deep theological truth, namely, that God speaks in silence. It is in the silence that the Holy Spirit does his most powerful work, making permanent what otherwise would have been evanescent; impressing truths as a potter makes an impress on clay; registering on mind and conscience what has just been said in words.

If this be true, what about the *end* of the sermon? Is not this, *above all*, the place for silence? Let me confess that for many years I used to end the sermon with the ascription: "Now to

God the Father, God the Son, and God the Holy Spirit be ascribed, as are most justly due, all might, majesty, dominion and power, now and for ever, Amen." I scarcely ever use these words now. Why? Because hardly anybody took any notice of them. They were an excuse for the members of the congregation to get to their feet, to find the money for the collection, or to think about going home. Further, it is unwise to announce the anthem or the hymn immediately after the end of the spoken word. Norman Goodall, in a lecture entitled *I Believe in Words*, made the point well: "How often, alas, is the saying verified that 'the preacher soweth the Word; then cometh the choir and taketh away that which hath been sown'!" Let me repeat: is not this the place for silence? Is not this the point where the Holy Spirit of truth must be given his opportunity to register, to imprint, to confute, to convict, to convince? The sermon ends, perhaps with a brief summary of what has been said. "Let us keep silence", says the preacher. It can be a moment of great power. Or "Let us pray"; and after a stillness, the briefest prayer takes up the point of the sermon and encapsulates what has been said. That is a climax much to be desired.

Brief silences such as I have indicated will not lead to dullness or boredom. Rather, the reverse. Carefully planned and used in a congregation well taught about them, they can be the creative moments of weekly worship. There is a power in silence, the very power of God.

✳

Let this book, then, itself go out into silence. But not before its author yields to the temptation to quote from a remarkable little book by Frederick Buechner. He is dealing with our theme — preacher, words, and silence: "Since words are his chief instrument, words are what he chiefly has to use but remembering always that the silence that his words frame — the silence that his words are born out of and that his words break and that his words are swallowed up by — may well convey the mystery of truth better than the words themselves can, just as the empty space inside a church may well convey better than all the art and architecture of a church the mystery of that in which we live and move and have our being. We put frames of words around silence and shells of stone and wood around emptiness, but it is the silence, the emptiness themselves, that finally matter and out of which the Gospel comes as word" (*Telling the Truth: The Gospel as Tragedy, Comedy and Fairy Tale*, p. 26).

> Lord, still me.
> Let my mind be enquiring, searching.
> Let my heart be open.
> Save me from mental rust.
> Deliver me from spiritual decay.
> Keep me *alive* and alert.
> Teach me, that I may teach them.
>
> Lord, give me the gifts
> to make this gift to you.
> (A prayer of St Augustine before preaching)

I Believe
Trevor Huddleston

A simple, prayerful series of reflections on the phrases of the Creed. This is a beautiful testament of the strong, quiet inner faith of a man best known for his active role in the Church – and in the world.

The Heart of the Christian Faith
Donald Coggan

The author ". . . presents the essential core of Christianity in a marvellously simple and readable form, quite uncluttered by any excess of theological technicality."
The Yorkshire Post

Be Still and Know
Michael Ramsey

The former Archbishop of Canterbury looks at prayer in the New Testament, at what the early mystics could teach us about it, and at some practical aspects of Christian praying.

Pilgrim's Progress
John Bunyan

"A masterpiece which generation after generation of ordinary men and women have taken to their hearts."
Hugh Ross Williamson

Also available in Fount Paperbacks

The Mind of St Paul
WILLIAM BARCLAY

'There is a deceptive simplicity about this fine exposition of Pauline thought at once popular and deeply theological. The Hebrew and Greek backgrounds are described and all the main themes are lightly but fully treated.'   *The Yorkshire Post*

The Plain Man Looks at the Beatitudes
WILLIAM BARCLAY

'. . . the author's easy style should render it . . . valuable and acceptable to the ordinary reader.'   *Church Times*

The Plain Man Looks at the Lord's Prayer
WILLIAM BARCLAY

Professor Barclay shows how this prayer that Jesus gave to his disciples is at once a summary of Christian teaching and a pattern for all prayers.

The Plain Man's Guide to Ethics
WILLIAM BARCLAY

The author demonstrates beyond all possible doubt that the Ten Commandments are the most relevant document in the world today and are totally related to mankind's capacity to live and make sense of it all within a Christian context.

Ethics in a Permissive Society
WILLIAM BARCLAY

How do we as Christians deal with such problems as drug taking, the 'pill', alcohol, morality of all kinds, in a society whose members are often ignorant of the Church's teaching? Professor Barclay approaches a difficult and vexed question with his usual humanity and clarity, asking what Christ himself would say or do in our world today.

BOOKS BY C. H. DODD

The Authority of the Bible

"In what sense, if in any, may the Bible still be regarded as authority, and how are we to interpret the authority of Christ? These are the questions to which Professor Dodd addresses himself . . ."

Expository Times

The Founder of Christianity

"A first-rate and fascinating book . . . a theological event."
Times Literary Supplement

The Meaning of Paul for Today

Professor Dodd particularly seeks to bring out the permanent significance of Paul's thought, in modern terms, and in relation to the general interests and problems which occupy the mind of the present generation.

The Parables of the Kingdom

"This book is a most thought-provoking . . . contribution to a very difficult subject."

Methodist Recorder

Also available in Fount Paperbacks

Yours Faithfully – Volume 1
GERALD PRIESTLAND

'There can be no doubt that Gerald Priestland has brought new life to the reporting of religious news. Nothing as good has happened to radio since Alistair Cooke started "Letter from America".'

Edwin Robertson, Baptist Times

Yours Faithfully – Volume 2
GERALD PRIESTLAND

'He is positive, informed, urbane, incisive, witty and unafraid. His speech is always with grace seasoned with salt . . .'

W. M. Macartney, Life and Work

Gerald Priestland at Large
GERALD PRIESTLAND

'This final collection of *Yours Faithfully* broadcast talks . . . is as apposite as it is humane and humorous . . . Gerald Priestland's usually wise and thoughtful opinions make this book a very good buy.'

Mary Endersbee, Today

Fount Paperbacks

Fount is one of the leading paperback publishers of religious books and below are some of its recent titles.

- [ ] GETHSEMANE Martin Israel £2.50
- [ ] HIS HEALING TOUCH Michael Buckley £2.50
- [ ] YES TO LIFE David Clarke £2.95
- [ ] THE DIVORCED CATHOLIC Edmund Flood £1.95
- [ ] THE WORLD WALKS BY Sue Masham £2.95
- [ ] C. S. LEWIS: THE MAN AND HIS GOD
      Richard Harries £1.75
- [ ] BEING FRIENDS Peter Levin £2.95
- [ ] DON'T BE AFRAID TO SAY YOU'RE LONELY
      Christopher Martin £2.50
- [ ] BASIL HUME: A PORTRAIT Tony Castle (ed.) £3.50
- [ ] TERRY WAITE: MAN WITH A MISSION
      Trevor Barnes £2.95
- [ ] PRAYING THROUGH PARADOX Charles Elliott £2.50
- [ ] TIMELESS AT HEART C. S. Lewis £2.50
- [ ] THE POLITICS OF PARADISE Frank Field £3.50
- [ ] THE WOUNDED CITY Trevor Barnes £2.50
- [ ] THE SACRAMENT OF THE WORD Donald Coggan £2.95
- [ ] IS THERE ANYONE THERE? Richard MacKenna £1.95

All Fount paperbacks are available through your bookshop or newsagent, or they can be ordered by post from Fount Paperbacks, Cash Sales Department, G.P.O. Box 29, Douglas, Isle of Man. Please send purchase price plus 22p per book, maximum postage £3. Customers outside the UK send purchase price, plus 22p per book. Cheque, postal order or money order. No currency.

NAME (Block letters)_____

ADDRESS _____

_____

_____